Ice Roses

Sarah Kirsch was born in 1935 in Saxony. One of Germany's leading ~~~~~~~ ~~~~, ~~~~~, ~~~~ published ten volumes of poetry and received numerous awards, including the Petrarch Prize (1976), the (West) German Critics' Prize (1981), and the Georg Büchner Prize (1996). She established her reputation in the former East Germany, moving to the West in 1977. Sarah Kirsch died on 5 May 2013.

Anne Stokes holds an MA in German from the University of Edinburgh and a PhD in German Literature from Ohio State University. Having worked in the fields of German Studies and English as a Foreign Language, she now works as a freelance translator. She recently completed a PhD in Creative Writing at the University of Glasgow.

Sarah Kirsch

Ice Roses
SELECTED POEMS

Selected, translated and introduced by
Anne Stokes

CARCANET

First published in Great Britain in 2014 by
Carcanet Press Limited
Alliance House
Cross Street
Manchester M2 7AQ

www.carcanet.co.uk

A CIP catalogue record for this book is available from the British Library

ISBN 978 1 84777 151 3

The publisher acknowledges financial assistance from Arts Council England

Supported by
ARTS COUNCIL
ENGLAND

Typeset by XL Publishing Services, Exmouth

Contents

CONTENTS   vii

From *Erlkönigs Tochter* (Alder King's Daughter)

From *Bodenlos* (Fathomless)

From *Schwanenliebe* (Swan Love)

Acknowledgements

For feedback on some of the translations, or quick answers to queries concerning the German, I would like to thank Ralf Banken, Anja Konig, Ray Stokes, and, above all, Evelyn Schlag.

I am also very much indebted to Michael Schmidt for offering to publish this book, and to the editors of *Poetry London* and *Modern Poetry in Translation* for featuring some of the translations in their journals.

Finally, I would like to thank Helen Tookey at Carcanet for her meticulous copy-editing. Needless to say, however, responsibility for any mistakes or omissions rests with me.

Introduction

Sarah Kirsch (1935–2013) was one of Germany's foremost lyric poets. Between 1967 and 2012 she published ten volumes of poetry and received numerous awards for her writing, including the Petrarch Prize (1976), the (West) German Critics' Prize (1981), and the prestigious Georg Büchner Prize (1996) awarded by the German Academy for Language and Literature. Although known mainly for her poetry, she also wrote prose, which she regarded as an extension of her poetic work, and she painted in watercolours, as a diversion from both.[1]

Despite her critical acclaim and notoriety, however, Kirsch, who embarked on her literary career in the former East Germany, which she was compelled to leave in the late seventies, opted from the early eighties to lead a very private life in a former schoolhouse in a small village in the northern province of Schleswig-Holstein, close to the Danish border.[2] After moving there, she rarely gave interviews,[3] but in 2005, on the occasion of her seventieth birthday, she made a rare foray into the public sphere by agreeing to discuss her work in her home with the younger Berlin poet Marion Poschmann (b. 1969) in the presence of the journalist Iris Radisch of *Die Zeit*. In the ensuing discussion, which was prompted and recorded by Radisch for the newspaper, Kirsch laconically ascribed her literary success to biographical misfortune: 'I was a child in the Nazi era. Then I became acquainted with the GDR, then West Germany, then the one they recently tossed together. You can't pack much more than that into a lifetime. My motto was always: A writer can't have it bad enough.'[4]

As a political non-conformist, Kirsch certainly had her share of adversity while resident in the former East Germany. Born Ingrid Hella Irmelinde Bernstein in 1935 in Limlingerode in Southern Saxony, an area which became part of the GDR in 1949, she took the name Kirsch when she married East German poet Rainer Kirsch in 1960, and, in the same year, she adopted the name Sarah in commemoration of Jewish victims of the Holocaust, thereby distancing herself from Fascism, and, more generally, highlighting the fact that anti-Semitism was a feature not only of West but also East Germany's past. Often at the centre of controversy because of the criticism of state policy implicit in much of her writing, Kirsch was finally forced to leave East Germany in 1977 owing to persecution she experienced after signing a petition against the expulsion of the non-conformist singer-songwriter Wolf Biermann in November of the previous year. Kirsch was one of the first signatories, and when she refused to withdraw her support for Biermann, immediate reprisals were taken against her. In December 1976, she was excluded from the Party and the Berlin section of the writers' association, and her third volume of poetry, which appeared in the same month, was consequently ignored. Thereafter, she was subjected to Stasi surveillance as well as harassment by the neighbours of the one-and-a-half-room flat she had occupied since moving to East Berlin following her divorce from Rainer Kirsch in 1968. 'Juden heraus' ('Jews out') was smeared on her door, and a notice requesting 'the lady on the 17th floor' to kindly leave was posted in the lobby. Not surprisingly, then, when she applied for an exit visa for herself and her seven-year-old son (whose father was the poet Karl Mickel, 1935–2000), permission was quickly granted. They moved to West Berlin in August 1977.[5]

Like Biermann, however, Kirsch had not always been disaffected with the East German state. Although an avid reader and writer of poetry in her teens, she was inspired by the vivid landscapes she discovered in the novels of the Austrian Romantic Adalbert Stifter to study not literature but forestry, followed by biology, so that she could contribute constructively to socialist society. She also worked in a sugar factory prior to becoming a student. 'You couldn't yet think about poetry,' she remarked to Poschmann in 2005.[6] It was while she was studying biology at the University of Halle, however, that she met Rainer Kirsch, and began to frequent a writing group with him and his circle of literary friends. The group, led by Gerhard Wolf, met for two days each month, and, as Kirsch recounted shortly after her arrival in the West, as a student of biology, she was able to embark on writing in the naive and advantageous belief that writing was easy, since, unlike the others, she was 'unburdened' by a detailed knowledge of German literature. Furthermore, she commented, Wolf also simplified the task by directing the fledgling writers away from philosophical issues, and encouraging them to write instead about things around them, things they really knew, like waking up, having breakfast, and going to the market in Halle.[7] After five years, provided one had been published, membership of this group then led automatically to membership of the writers' association, which, in turn, provided access to a writing scholarship. Consequently, shortly after joining the association, and gaining some experience on a couple of collective farms, Kirsch studied writing at the Johannes R. Becher Institut für Literatur in Leipzig.

Study at the Leipzig institute from 1963 to 1965 was extremely important to the development of Kirsch as a poet. In a seminar led by the poet, essayist and translator Georg Maurer, Kirsch and her contemporaries – including the poets Karl Mickel, Richard Leising and Heinz Czechowski – developed a sense of their writing in relation to German literary precedents. Maurer, for instance, Kirsch recalled in 1979, encouraged them to measure their own nature poems against those of Barthold Heinrich Brockes (an eighteenth-century poet and translator whose poetry was characterised by precise and analytical observation of nature and a clear, simple diction) and the nineteenth-century writer and composer Annette von Droste-Hülshoff (whose keen sensory perception and precise recording of natural phenomena positioned her between Romanticism and Realism).[8] Indeed, on account of the thematisation of and emotional response to love, nature, and politics in Kirsch's poetry, the German critic Marcel Reich-Ranicki later referred to her as 'Drostes jüngere Schwester' [Droste's younger sister].[9] Kirsch considered herself a successor to Droste-Hülshoff and Bettina von Armin, and addresses both in her 1973 volume *Zaubersprüche* (Incantations; 'Wiepensdorfer-Zyklus No. 9', not included in this selection, and 'Der Droste würde ich gern Wasser reichen', 'I would gladly hold a candle to Droste', pp. 36/37),[10] which was described by Adolf Endler as the most freely sexual or erotic volume ever produced by a significant female German poet.[11]

While studying in Leipzig, moreover, Kirsch was also influenced by world literature available only in the institute's library, or acquired from West Germany. Through Enzensberger's

Museum der modernen Poesie (Museum of Modern Poetry, published in West Germany in 1960, and sent to her by friends in the West) as well as Erich Arendt's Colombian poetry and the latter's translations of Rafael Alberti, for example, she discovered that a poem did not have to be openly agitational to be directly and eminently political.[12] The graphic imagery of Alberti, the German Modernist poets Paul Celan and Ingeborg Bachman, and the Russian poet Anna Akhmatova, whose work Kirsch translated into German, also had a profound influence on the young poet-painter.[13] Like Bachmann and Celan, moreover, Kirsch, too, thematised the Holocaust.[14] But while these poets found language increasingly inadequate to deal with this subject, Kirsch did not. The leitmotif of the threat of annihilation and the apocalyptic tone of much of her work have, however, been ascribed to her preoccupation with the Holocaust,[15] and her refusal to conform to German rules of syntax, which I discuss below, could perhaps also be related to her condemnation of it.

As a result of these and other influences, while Kirsch's first volume, *Gespräch mit dem Saurier* (Conversation with the Saurian), co-authored with Rainer Kirsch and published in 1965, was heavily indebted to the dictates of Socialist Realism both formally and thematically, a singular and original poetic voice was already evident in her first solo volume, *Landaufenthalt*[16] (A Stay in the Country), which appeared only two years later.

Looking back on Kirsch's poetic achievement in 1991, fellow poet Heinz Czechowski asserted that *Landaufenthalt* 'simply confirmed what her friends and readers already knew: with Sarah's poems a new tone had entered German lyric poetry'.[17] More specifically, as Martin Kane has pointed out, compared with the rather simplistic rhyming poems contained in *Gespräch mit dem Saurier*, those that comprise *Landaufenthalt* are characterised by the 'virtual abandonment of rhyme, and a much more adventurous use of elliptical narrative and enjambement, punctuation and syntax'.[18] As the opening poem, 'By the white daisies' (which also opens this selection), demonstrates, Kirsch uses sparse descriptive language, incorporating speech cadences and colloquialisms, and virtually free of conjunctions and punctuation, particularly commas, in which German abounds, to produce poetry with a casual tone and a sense of immediacy and directness. In addition to these formal differences, moreover, critics also discerned a thematic shift in her first solo volume: while nature and love still loom large, Kirsch's nature and love poems now 'yield social and historical perspectives',[19] which, for the most part, 'arise unexpectedly and indirectly out of an intensely personal experience'.[20] The 'socialist reality' of sexual equality, for instance, is subtly questioned in 'By the white daisies'. In short, then, while this first solo collection still contains expressions of affection for and loyalty to the socialist state, Kirsch, like the other East German 'Neue Welle' ('New Wave') poets with whom she studied in Leipzig, was now expressing her personal experience of life in the collective – in her case, as a woman – in ways that were incompatible with Socialist Realism.

Naturally, though, this development did not sit well with orthodox East German critics. Rainer Kirsch, for instance, was not granted his writing diploma.[21] And, in 1968, poetry by him and other young poets collected in an anthology titled *Saison für Lyrik: Neue Gedichte von siebzehn Autoren* (Poetry Season: New Poems by Seventeen Authors)[22] was condemned by conservative critics as socially distanced and fatalistic, and two of Sarah Kirsch's poems, 'Grünes Land' ('Green Land') and 'Weites Haus' ('Faraway House'), were singled out as examples.[23] Similar criticism, moreover, was levelled against her poetry of the late sixties and seventies, which frequently contained fantastical or fairytale elements, ridiculed conformist behaviours, and expressed unrest or longing (for the ability to travel beyond East Germany's heavily guarded borders, for instance) on the part of female personae, who, in their consistency, appear to be synonymous with the poet herself. Most notably, her poem 'Schwarze Bohnen' ('Black beans', pp. 24/25) – the despondent response of a woman as she waits in vain for her lover – was singled out at the Sixth Writers' Congress in 1969 as overly subjective and negative. Four years later, however, in the wake of Erich Honecker's 'no taboos' speech of 1972, the same poem was held up at the Seventh Writers' Congress as an example of socialist writing that encapsulated the complexities and contradictions of socialist life.[24]

As the varied reception of 'Schwarze Bohnen' ('Black beans') indicates, throughout the seventies East German cultural policy switched back and forth in terms of openness, but during this time Kirsch held her course. The most likely reason for this, she commented during her discussion with Poschmann in 2005, was that she did not believe that she ever had a choice as to how she expressed herself. From an early stage in her poetic development, she claimed, she had quite simply been unable to write generally and optimistically about the future of the socialist state, or to relinquish the first-person pronoun 'ich' ('I'). Writing in the first person, she elaborated, had, in fact, been her salvation. Indeed, in the early seventies, Kirsch even wrote a poem titled 'Ich' ('Me', pp. 40/41), and the 'I' of this and other poems, as Poschmann pointed out, in addition to being courageous (in the East German context), always takes a position, has its point of view and an overview. This is true even of her love poems, which are often expressions of dissatisfaction or abandonment, since the absolute love Kirsch's female personae seek is rarely reciprocated, a fact which possibly led Kirsch to state at seventy that she hoped never to fall in love again.[25] But although her poetic personae frequently express the emotional turmoil accompanying abandonment or betrayal, they do not languish in the role of victim. Instead, anxiety and sadness are ultimately reined in by humour or self-irony.[26] Her writing thus functioned as an act of catharsis.

Kirsch's highly subjective work, which frequently took a critical or satirical stance towards the East German state, was well received by her compatriots. By the time she left the GDR in the late seventies, she was without doubt one of East Germany's leading poets.[27] Her reputation had been secured not only by *Landaufenthalt* (A Stay in the Country, 1967), but, in the wake of Honecker's 'no taboos' speech, by *Zaubersprüche* (Incantations, 1973), in which the poems 'Schwarze Bohnen' ('Black beans') and 'Ich' ('Me') appeared, and *Rückenwind* (Tailwind, 1976). All three volumes, moreover, were published in West Germany shortly after they appeared in the East, and her debut volume was reissued soon after her arrival in the West.[28] Indeed, it was this, combined with the circumstance that Kirsch was still living in a German-speaking country, that led her to say in a

1979 interview that she did not feel like an exile in West Berlin, but that she was nonetheless saddened by the fact that her work was no longer being published in the East, although some of it, she knew, would get through. 'I haven't lost all my readers there,' she remarked, adding, 'in West Germany, I have many readers, even if they have quite different motives.'[29]

One of the motives was, of course, the tendency of Western readers and critics to look for political meanings even in poems that are not on the face of it concerned with socio-political issues. When questioned by Radisch about the validity of this preoccupation, Kirsch responded that her work was never overtly political, but that a certain consciousness and particular conditions that characterised her as a GDR citizen had, of course, found their way into it.[30] Later in the same interview, however, Kirsch said that it was her intention to write about people, and that while people are political objects, they are not exclusively so.[31] Indeed, despite the political allusions discernible in her work, it is not politics but, above all, love and nature – and often both together – that are the poet's central and enduring concerns, as became clear after she left the politically charged East German context.

The main impetuses for her writing, Kirsch explained in 1979, were visual stimuli that called forth a line, and uncovered something that had been stored.[32] The catalysts for her poetry were what she saw in front of her, on the street, flickering past occasionally on TV, or, more often than not, in the natural world.[33] In her poems, Kirsch emerges as a keen observer of nature and the sensations and associations it evoked in her. 'My poems always had something to do with landscape… Since I was ten, I've known that I have to live in a beautiful place', she told *Die Zeit* in 2005. 'I go somewhere and graze on everything there. It was already like that in my first volume, *Landaufenthalt*. It's optical impressions that trigger something in me. I see something and I want to capture exactly what it looked like. What effect it had. What I felt. How the wind sounded. What the colour was. There is actually only ever one correct solution, as with a crossword, and I've got to get as close to it as possible. That can take me days, it's a quest.'

Kirsch's early poems, imitations of the young Goethe written in school notebooks when she was fourteen, recorded impressions garnered from her parents' garden and the surrounding countryside at the edge of the Harz Mountains. She later recalled, however, that even as a child she already wanted to experience more.[34] After leaving East Germany for West Berlin – a move she made willingly, she claimed two years later, since the political attention she received prior to her departure was distracting her from her work, and had deprived her of the 'looseness and lightness' ('Lockerheit und Leichtigkeit') she required to be creative[35] – Kirsch travelled extensively in Italy, France and the United States, 'conquering' the places she visited by writing about them.[36] In the early eighties, however, she settled in an old schoolhouse in the remote village of Tielenhemme in Schleswig-Holstein, and, after that, the sparsely populated, stark landscape of this area – marked by fens, marshes, tidal basins, and the screams of geese – dominated her work.

In Kirsch's last interview, the one granted *Die Zeit* in 2005, the poet, who routinely gave public readings into the eighties, but later preferred to communicate through her writing, explained that, at the age of 48, after returning from the plains and deserts of America, she made a snap decision to leave West Berlin, in order to be closer to nature. And, after a short stay in a village near Bremen, she moved on to Schleswig-Holstein, and quickly became attached to the area. 'I must describe everything here, it's like I've taken on that task,' she explained. 'I'm grazing on everything here like a sheep, eating it all up until there's nothing left.' Nor did she envisage completing the task any time soon: 'Remarkably, I can describe the same thing again and again from different angles. I've already written so many poems here. Then, in my last volume, *Schwanenliebe* (Swan Love), I suddenly wrote these short haiku-like things, in which I basically presented everything again, from a different angle. When you know something really well, have absorbed it to such an extent that you can reproduce it in two lines, it's really very satisfying. Even my daily notes are essentially the same, but they always take different turns. It's just like life, the same and yet not the same. You need to have humility and modesty.'

Like love, however, nature in Kirsch's work is far from idyllic; indeed, in the light of the signs of ecological devastation evident in her later poems, it is, arguably, above all the biologist's detailed descriptions of ecological damage and loss that lend her poetry contemporary as well as historical significance. Back in 2005, however, Kirsch was keen to stress that she did not write 'nature poetry' in a strict sense, and that she was not a detached, scientific observer; her experience of the external world was often in fact entwined with what was going on inside her: 'Perhaps nature poetry [is an appropriate term] if it means seeing yourself as part of nature. Trees and clouds also express your state of mind. It is all interconnected. When you're happy, really happy, then you see beauty. If I'm in my car and I suddenly see two swans flying across a clear-blue sky, I'm so happy, because it's so beautiful that I don't care where I'm going... [But] you have to be able to see beauty.' Kirsch, in other words, did not merely describe nature; she discovered in it correlatives of her psychological or emotional states. Her nature poetry, moreover, is not environmental in a polemical sense. When asked at seventy if she believed in nature, she responded: 'I'm not devout, but I believe in many things. I believe in trees rather than God. I have faith in the many deities inherent in things. I believe in those who lived before us.' Alongside human beings, trees, plants, birds, animals, and angels populate her poetic landscapes, which, in addition to conveying the poet's state of mind, inform her readers indirectly of the beauty and fragility of nature, and humankind's capacity for its destruction and responsibility for its protection and recovery.

The following selection of poems, arranged chronologically, is taken from the *Sämtliche Gedichte* (Collected Poems) issued by Kirsch's publishing house, the Deutsche Verlags-Anstalt, in 2005 to mark her seventieth birthday, and is representative of the range and expressiveness of her poetry from the appearance of her first solo volume in East Germany in 1967 until 2001, when her last volume of verse appeared. This selection does not, therefore, include poems from the 1965 volume *Gespräch mit dem Saurier* (Conversation with the Saurian) that the poet co-authored with Rainer Kirsch, since she later distanced herself from this work,[37] and requested that the poems not be included in the Collected Poems.[38] Included are poems from the three volumes she wrote while resident in the GDR (*Landaufenthalt* [A Stay in the Country, 1967], *Zaubersprüche* [Incantations, 1973] and *Rückenwind* [Tailwind, 1976]), as well as from her eight later volumes (*Drachensteigen* [Kite Flying, 1979]; *Erdreich* [Earth, 1982]; *Katzenleben* [Cat Lives, 1984]; *Schneewärme* [Snow Warmth, 1989]; *Erlkönigs Tochter* [Alder King's Daughter, 1992]; *Bodenlos* [Fathomless, 1996] and *Schwanenliebe* [Swan Love, 2001]).[39] The sparse, meditative, often sombre and fragmentary verse of the last two volumes, which differs markedly from the breathless, emotionally charged poetry of her earlier collections, has not been translated previously.

The main themes of Kirsch's work are represented here: the vicissitudes of love; Germany's Nazi past and the Holocaust; personal experience of life in the former East Germany, and, later, in the West, although not necessarily in that order;[40] and, latterly, humanity's relationship with nature, which is of topical interest in Britain, as reflected, for instance, in recent poetry by Kathleen Jamie and Alice Oswald. These subjects, however, seldom appear in isolation in Kirsch's poems. The ninth poem from the Wiepersdorf-Zyklus (Wiepersdorf-cycle) contained in *Rückenwind* (Tailwind, 1976), for example, which does not feature in this selection, speaks of anxiety related to awaiting a lover and/or to the possible presence of Stasi informants:

> *This evening, Bettina, things are*
> *As they've always been. We are*
> *Always alone when writing*
> *To our kings.*
> *Those of the heart and*
> *Those of the state. And yet*
> *Our hearts start*
> *When we hear a car*
> *On the street.*

And, in the poem 'Selektion' (pp. 112/113), the Holocaust and human manipulation of nature are both present. In fact, it was the complex intermingling of these two themes in that poem that first attracted me to Kirsch's verse as a PhD student of German literature in the late eighties, and which led me to re-engage with her work when her collected poems appeared around 20 years later. As a creative writing student at that time, moreover, I was also drawn to formal qualities of Kirsch's free verse, which I believe will interest an English-speaking poetry audience. As Joachim Kaiser pointed out in 1995 in his introduction to a retrospective of Kirsch's poetry, the enduring quality of Kirsch's poems is not so much their content as their music.[41] What the West German writer and critic Peter Hacks dubbed the 'Sarah sound' in the sixties[42] is characterised by a sense of flow attained through minimal use of punctuation and by a sliding syntax in which the final part of one clause often co-serves as the start of the next. Also, although Kirsch's use of punctuation does vary, commas (when used at all) generally separate out ideas or different geographical or temporal spaces, rather than serving the usual grammatical function in German of dividing clauses. Many of her poems, moreover, end with a full stop, even if no other punctuation is present. And speech cadences and colloquialisms, with the odd anachronistic phrase or neologism thrown in as stumbling blocks,[43] are also key features of her poetics.

The sense of casualness and the ambiguities that result from Kirsch's diction and syntax were undoubtedly expedient features of critical verse produced and published within the ideological confines of the GDR. After Kirsch moved to the West, however, these elements remained essential aspects of her style. As she indicated in the early eighties, at a basic level her punctuation offers a guide to how she wants the poems to be read: 'breathlessly, without breaking off so that each word has the same value, and reaches over to the right and to the left, not only in terms of meaning'.[44] More fundamentally, though, as she stated in 1997, she believes that 'omitting punctuation also brings freedom. It makes many readings possible. Grammar, too, expresses the soul.'[45]

Kirsch's free-flowing lines could thus be interpreted as an expression of the poet's unwillingness to be fettered by rules of any kind, while the grammar of her poems also frequently functions to merge the inner and outer worlds, the poet and her social and natural surroundings. Despite their fluidity, however, the poems are, of course, not entirely without formal properties, and, in aiming to produce poems in English of similar or approximate value to the German originals, I have attempted as far as possible not only to capture the alliteration, rhythm and tone of Kirsch's free verse, but to adhere to a basic organising principle of her poems: the tendency to produce harmonious line endings via assonantal rhyme.

Previous translators of Kirsch's poetry have remarked on the challenges the poet's idiosyncratic syntax poses for the reader and translator. However, as Marina Roscher pointed out in her introduction to her co-translation of Kirsch's 1984 volume *Katzenleben* (*Cat Lives*), comprehension is greatly aided by the clear visual descriptions the poems contain. Consequently, Roscher and others have generally opted to render Kirsch's texts in English as close to the German original as possible, and I have attempted to do the same. There are, however, fundamental differences between German and English syntax; thus, in contrast to some of the previous translators (for the most part Germanists concerned above all with the political content of Kirsch's work), I have, while observing the poet's minimal use of punctuation, frequently altered the order of the sentences so that what does not sound strange to the German ear is not made strange through word-for-word translation.

I have not, however, attempted to explain or clarify in English anything that is deliberately left ambiguous in the German, although I have, on occasion, changed the denotative meaning of the German slightly, in order to uphold thematic imagery, or to approximate formal principles or sound values in English – in short, to achieve dynamic or functional equivalence.[46] In 'Journey I' (p. 5), for example, 'Schwertlilien' in the original are actually 'irises' in English, but I have translated the term as 'sword lilies', a type of gladiolus, to maintain the war imagery contained in the original. Similarly, in 'The air already smells like snow' (p. 47), while 'Eisblumen' equates to 'frost work' or 'frost patterns', I have instead opted for a literal translation, 'ice flowers', as this is more in keeping with the romantic theme of the poem. Changes made for the maintenance of formal or sound patterning include the following. In 'The night extends its fingers' (p. 27), I have translated the German 'Baum', which means 'tree' in English, as 'bush' to produce assonance with 'room' and 'ruin' to compensate for the assonance present in the

German between 'Baum' and 'Raum' ('room'). In 'All-kinds-of-fur' (p. 67), the German 'halb nach vier', which means 'half past four', has been changed to 'half three' to create assonance with 'machines' (and 'screams'), as in the German between 'Maschinen' and 'vier'. And in 'The exercise' (pp. 101–103), the date 1905, which assonates in the original with the word for door in the following line, has been altered in my English version to 1904, since the date itself has no apparent significance, and the change enabled a similar sound effect in English.

More generally, though, in rendering Kirsch's German poems as poems in English, I have attempted, as far as is possible in translation, not only to reproduce the aesthetic qualities of the originals but to retain as much of their semantic content as possible. As Stanley Kunitz wrote in 'A Note on the Translations' which prefaces his *Poems of Akhmatova*, however, 'translation is a sum of approximations',[47] so, inevitably, in addition to the above shifts, many difficult linguistic and aesthetic choices had to be made along the way. Still, at some point, it is necessary to call a halt to the decision-making. In 'Freie Verse' ('Free verse', pp. 196/197), the final poem of *Erlkönigs Töchter* (Alder King's Daughter), Kirsch writes of how she felt compelled to release her poems to her German readers after a few years in her safe keeping. It is my hope that these selected translations of her poems, which have been in my safe keeping for a number of years, will, as a complement to previous translations, finally bring the sense and sound of her verse to the wider Anglophone audience it deserves. I put them forward with Sarah Kirsch's permission to interpret her words as I see fit.[48] And I would like to dedicate the work to her memory.

Notes

1   Stated in interview by Mererid Hopwood and Annette Zimmermann titled 'Fragen hinter der Tür: Gespräch mit Sarah Kirsch', in *Sarah Kirsch*, ed. Mererid Hopwood and David Basker (Cardiff: University of Wales Press, 1997), p. 11.
2   Stated in report by Brita Janssen, 'Sarah Kirsch zum 75. Geburtstag', *Die Berliner Zeitung Online*, 16 April 2010, http://www.bz-berlin.de/kultur/literatur/sarah-kirsch-zum-75-Geburtstag-article808698.html. (Accessed 1 October 2010.)

3   On 22 May 2013, the *Voralberger Nachrichten* cited a comment she made to the *Stuttgarter Nachrichten* in 1996: 'Die Leute sollen meine Gedichte gern haben und mich möglichst in Ruhe lassen' ('People should like my poems and leave me in peace as far as possible').

4   See interview with Iris Radisch titled 'Mann muss demütig und einfach sein', *Die Zeit Online*, 14 April 2005, No. 16, http://www.zeit.de/2005/16/L-Kirsch-Gespr_8ach. (Accessed 1 October 2010.)

5   See Mererid Hopkins, 'Sarah Kirsch: Outline Biography', and Martin Kane, '"...aus der ersten Hälfte meines Landes": Sarah Kirsch in the GDR', in Hopwood and Basker (ed.), *Sarah Kirsch*, p. 29.

6   Stated in *Die Zeit* interview.

7   Gerhardt Wolf, the husband of the prominent (East) German novelist Christa Wolf, worked as a literary critic, script-writer, and above all as an editor and promoter of young poets in East Germany in the 1960s.

8   Kirsch speaks of his influence in 'Ein Gespräch mit Sarah Kirsch', interview conducted by Hans Ester and Dick van Stekelenburg on 3 May 1979, first published in the yearbook *Deutsche Bücher*, vol. IX (1979), pp. 102–13, and reprinted in *Sarah Kirsch: Hundert Gedichte* (Ebenhausen bei München: Langewiesche-Brandt, 1985), pp. 123–34.

9   Reported in *Der Spiegel*, 22 May 2013.

10 Stated by Wulf Segebrecht, *Frankfurter Allgemeine Zeitung*, 22 May 2013.

11 Cited in *Der Spiegel*, 22 May 2013. Endler (1930–2009) was a poet, prose writer and essayist who supported the avant-garde literary scene in East Germany until the fall of the Wall in 1989.

12 Ester and van Stekelenburg, 'Ein Gespräch mit Sarah Kirsch'.

13 Barbara Mabee, *Die Poetik von Sarah Kirsch: Erinnerungsarbeit und Geschichtsbewußtsein* (Amsterdam: Rodopi, 1989), pp. 25–26.

14 Kirsch's compound titles are also reminiscent of Celan's, and in the final lines of her poem 'Erdrauch' ('Terrestrial smoke', pp. 120–121) she also makes reference to the German-Jewish poet Nelly Sachs's volume *In den Wohnungen des Todes* (Berlin: Aufbau Verlag, 1947).

15 Mabee, *Die Poetik von Sarah Kirsch*, p. 12.

16 Kane, 'Sarah Kirsch in the GDR', p. 17.

17 Cited in German by Kane: ibid., p. 16.

18 Ibid., p. 17.

19 Ibid.

20 Ibid., p. 19.

21 Ester and van Stekelenburg, ' Ein Gespräch mit Sarah Kirsch', p. 124.

22 Edited by Joachim Schreck (Berlin: Aufbau, 1968).

23 Kane, 'Sarah Kirsch in the GDR', p. 21.

24 For a summary of the poet's reception in the sixties and seventies, see Kane, 'Sarah Kirsch in the GDR', pp. 20–22.

25 Stated in *Die Zeit* interview.

26 This point is made also by Kane, 'Sarah Kirsch in the GDR', pp. 23–25.

27 Her popularity is attested to by the fact that the house in which she was born was converted into a 'Dichterstätte' (poets' centre) in 2002, and Kirsch often attended readings there. Reported on MDR radio station on 22 May 2013.

28 Her first volume had appeared in the West in slightly expanded form as *Gedichte* in 1969.

29 Ester and van Stekelenburg, 'Ein Gespräch mit Sarah Kirsch', p. 128.

30 Ibid., p. 129.
31 Ibid., p. 130.
32 Ibid., p. 132.
33 Stated in *Die Zeit* interview.
34 Ibid.
35 Ester and van Stekelenburg, 'Ein Gespräch mit Sarah Kirsch', p. 130.
36 Ibid., p. 129.
37 Kane, 'Sarah Kirsch in the GDR', p. 14.
38 Kirsch's express wish that this work not be included in the collected volume is indicated in a note from the editor on the final page.
39 See bibliography for full publication details.
40 Kirsch, naturally, processed some of her experiences in East Germany after she moved to the West. Also, as Wulf Segebrecht pointed out in the *Frankfurter Allgemeine Zeitung* on 22 May 2013, the end of the GDR did not mean the end of her public disapproval of any form of conformism. In 1992, for example, she declined to accept her election to the Berlin Akademie der Künste (Academy of Arts) on the grounds that it was a hangout (*Schlumpfbude*) for former state poets and Stasi informers whom she did not want anything to do with.
41 Joachim Kaiser, 'Sarah Kirschs Gedichte', introduction to *Ich Crusoe: Sechzig Gedichte und sechs Aquarelle der Autorin* (Stuttgart: Deutsche Verlags-Anstalt, 1995), p. 13.
42 Cited by Michael Butler, '"Die Endlichkeit dieser Erde...": Sarah Kirsch's Chronicles of Transience', in Hopwood and Basker (ed.), *Sarah Kirsch*, p. 46.
43 Reference to stumbling blocks (*Stolpersteine*) comes from *Der Spiegel*, 22 May 2013.
44 Butler, '"Die Endlichkeit dieser Erde..."', p. 46.
45 Cited in Hopwood and Zimmermann interview, in Hopwood and Basker (ed.), *Sarah Kirsch*, p. 11.
46 The term 'dynamic equivalence' derives from Eugene Nida, *The Theory and Practice of Translation* (Leiden: E.J. Brill, 1969), and refers to sense-for-sense rather than word-for-word translation, with the aim of producing effects for the reader of the translated text analogous to those produced by the original text.
47 Stanley Kunitz with Max Hayward, *Poems of Akhmatova* (New York: Mariner Books, 1997), p. 32.
48 Kirsch requested and approved a sample of my translations via her German editor. She chose not to comment on queries I submitted to her editor, but said I was free to interpret as required.

Bibliography

Works by Sarah Kirsch

Landaufenthalt (East Berlin and Weimar: Aufbau Verlag, 1967; Ebenhausen bei München: Langewiesche-Brandt, 1977).
Gedichte (Ebenhausen bei München: Langewiesche-Brandt, 1969). [This volume consists mainly of poems contained in *Landaufenthalt*.]
Zaubersprüche (East Berlin and Weimar: Aufbau Verlag, 1973; Ebenhausen bei München: Langewiesche-Brandt, 1974).
Rückenwind (East Berlin and Weimar: Aufbau Verlag, 1976; Ebenhausen bei München: Langewiesche-Brandt, 1977).
Drachensteigen (Munich: Ebenhausen bei München: Langewiesche-Brandt, 1979).
Erdreich (Munich: Deutsche Verlags-Anstalt, 1982).
Katzenleben (Munich: Deutsche Verlags-Anstalt, 1984).
Hundert Gedichte (Ebenhausen bei München: Langewiesche-Brandt, 1985)
Schneewärme (Munich: Deutsche Verlags-Anstalt, 1989).
Erlkönigs Tochter (Munich: Deutsche Verlags-Anstalt, 1992).
Bodenlos (Munich: Deutsche Verlags-Anstalt, 1996).
Schwanenliebe (Munich: Deutsche Verlags-Anstalt, 2001).
Sämtliche Gedichte (Munich: Deutsche Verlags-Anstalt, 2005).

Works by Sarah Kirsch and Rainer Kirsch

Gespräch mit dem Saurier (Berlin: Neues Leben, 1965).

English translations

Hamburger, Michael, *German Poetry 1910–1975* (Manchester: Carcanet, 1977).
Hamburger, Michael (ed.), *An Anthology of East German Poetry* (Manchester: Carcanet, 1972).
Kvam, Wayne (ed. and trans.), *Conjurations: The Poems of Sarah Kirsch* (Athens, OH: Ohio University Press, 1985).
Lehbert, Margit (ed. and trans.), *Winter Poems* (London: Anvil, 1994).
Mulfold, Wendy and Anthony Vivis (ed. and trans.), *The Brontës' Hats* (Cambridge: First Street Editions, 1991).

Mulfold, Wendy and Anthony Vivis (ed. and trans.), *T* (Cambridge: Reality Street Editions, 1995).

Roscher, Marina and Charles Fishman (ed. and trans.) *Catlives: Sarah Kirsch's 'Katzenleben'* (Texas: Texas Tech University Press, 1991).

From

Landaufenthalt
(A Stay in the Country)

Bei den weißen Stiefmütterchen

Bei den weißen Stiefmütterchen
Im Park wie ers mir auftrug
Stehe ich unter der Weide
Ungekämmte Alte blattlos
Siehst du sagt sie er kommt nicht

Ach sage ich er hat sich den Fuß gebrochen
Eine Gräte verschluckt, eine Straße
Wurde plötzlich verlegt oder
Er kann seiner Frau nicht entkommen
Viele Dinge hindern uns Menschen

Die Weide wiegt sich und knarrt
Kann auch sein er ist schon tot
Sah blaß aus als er dich untern Mantel küßte
Kann sein Weide kann sein
So wollen wir hoffen er liebt mich nicht mehr

By the white daisies

By the white daisies
In the park I stand
Underneath the willow as he instructed me
Unkempt old woman without leaves
See she says he isn't coming

Och I say he's broken his foot
Choked on a fishbone, a street
Was suddenly moved or
He can't get away from his wife
Many things detain us human beings

The willow sways and creaks
May even be he's croaked
Looked pale when he was kissing you under your coat,
May be willow may be
Then let's hope he doesn't love me any more

Fahrt I

Die Erde in unserer Gegend ist übel dran
Der Winter wie Krieg ging seine Fetzen
Verdrecktes Verbandzeug zerfallen, da sehn
Narben und Schorf hervor, die Erde
In unserer Gegend ist grindig

Filziges bleiches Gras Schamhaar
Reckt sich über die größten Löcher, die Erde
Ist tonig sanft blutig stöhnt unterm trocknen Himmel

Die durchsichtigen Bäume sind so leicht zu verletzen
Daß sie ganz still stehn Modelle aus Glas

Nur Schwertlilien im Banhwärtergarten
Schlagen sich unbeirrt aus der Erde
Die Blattspitzen zerreißen dabei
Die ersten haben es am schwersten

Journey 1

The land in our parts is in a bad way
The winter was like war its rags
Filthy bandages are falling apart, and
Scars and scab are visible, the ground
Round here is scurfy

Felted pale grass pubic hair
Stretches across the largest gaps, the soil
Is clayey soft bloody moans beneath an arid sky

The diaphanous trees are so sensitive
They stand stock-still models of glass

Only sword lilies in the signalman's garden
Battle undeterred from the earth
In the process their leaf tips rip
The first ones have it the worst

Legende über Lilja

1
Ob sie schön war ist nicht zu verbürgen zumal
Die Aussagen der überlebenden Lagerbewohner
Sich widersprechen schon die Farbe des Haars
Unterschiedlich benannt wird in der Kartei
Sich kein Bild fand sie soll
Aus Polen geschickt worden sein

2
Im Sommer ging Lilja barfuß wie im Winter und schrieb
Sieben Briefe

3
Sechs drahtdünne Röllchen wandern
Durch Häftlingskittel übern Appellplatz kleben
An müder Haut stören den Schlaf erreichen
Den man nicht kennt (er kann nicht
Zeuge sein beim Prozeß)

4
Das siebente gab einer gegen Brot

5
Lilja in der Schreibstube Lilja unterwegs Lilja im Bunker
Schlag mit der Peitsche den Namen warum sagt sie nichts wer
weiß das
Warum schweigt sie im August wenn die Vögel
Singen im Rauch

Legend about Lilja

1

Whether she was pretty is uncertain since
The camp survivors' testimonies
Contradict each other even her hair colour
Is described in different ways in the index
No photo was found it was said
She had been sent from Poland

2

In summer as in winter Lilja went barefoot and composed
Seven letters

3

Six little wire-thin scrolls make their way
Under prison overalls across the roll-call square
Stick to tired skin disturb the sleep reach
The one no one knows (he cannot
Serve as a witness at the trial)

4

Someone gave the seventh up for bread

5

Lilja in the orderly room Lilja on her way Lilja in the bunker
Crack of the whip the name why does she say nothing
Who knows
Why's she schtum in August when the birds
Sing in the smoke

6
Einer mit Uniform Totenkopf am Kragen Liebhaber
Alter Theaterstücke (sein Hund mit klassischem Namen) erfand
Man sollte ihre Augen reden lassen

7
Durch die gefangenen Männer wurde eine Straße gemacht
Eine seltsame Allee geplünderter Bäume tat sich da auf
Hier sollte sie gehen und einen verraten

8
Nun brauch deine Augen Lilja befiehl
Den Muskeln dem Blut Sorglosigkeit hier bist du oft gegangen
Kennst jeden Stein jeden
Stein

9
Ihr Gesicht ging vorbei
Sagten die Überlebenden sie
Hätten gezittert Lilja wie tot ging ging
Bis der Mann dessen Hund Hamlet hieß
Brüllte befahl genug

10
Seitdem wurde sie nicht mehr gesehen

11
Andere Zeugen sagten sie habe auf ihrem Weg
Alle angelächelt sich mit den Fingern gekämmt
Sei gleich ins Gas gekommen – das war
Über zwanzig Jahr her –

6
A man in uniform death's head on his collar lover of
Old theatre plays (his dog had a classical name) thought
They should let her eyes give her away

7
A path was made through the captive males
A strange street of ravaged trees appeared
For her to pass through and betray someone

8
Use your eyes now Lilja command
Your muscles your blood to relax you've often gone this way
You know each stone each
Stone

9
Her face passed by
Survivors said they trembled
Lilja walked as if dead kept on going
Till the man with the dog called Hamlet
Roared ordered enough

10
After that she wasn't seen again

11
Other witnesses claimed that as she passed
She smiled at everyone, combed her fingers through her hair
Went straight into the gas – that was
Over twenty years ago –

12
Alle sprachen lange von Lilja

13
Die Richter von Frankfurt ließen im Jahr 65 protokollieren
Offensichtlich
Würden Legenden erzählt dieser Punkt
Sei aus der Anklage zu streichen

14
In dem Brief soll gestanden haben wir
Werden hier nicht rauskommen wir haben
Zu viel gesehn

12
For a long time they all spoke of Lilja

13
In '65 the court in Frankfurt minuted
It was evident
Legends were created this section
Should be struck from the accusation

14
The letter allegedly stated we
Won't get out of here we've
Seen too much

Ich in der Sonne deines Sterbemonats

Ich in der Sonne deines Sterbemonats
Ich im geöffneten Fenster
Ich betreibe Gewohntes: trockne
Gewaschenes Haar

Schaukeln fliegen
Am Augenwinkel vorbei, Wespen
Stelzen auf faulenden Birnen
Augesichts weißer Laken
Schreit der Wäschereihund: er ist noch klein

Flieg Haar von meinem Kamm
Flieg zwischen Spinnenfäden
Schwarzes Haar totes Haar
Eben noch bei mir

Me in the sun of the month you died

Me in the sun of the month you died
Me in the open window
Me doing ordinary things: Drying
My washed hair

Swings fly by
The corner of my eye, wasps
Totter on rotting pears
The laundry dog bawls
At the sight of white sheets: he is still small

Fly hair from my comb
Fly among spider-threads
Black hair dead hair
With me still a moment ago

Rückkunft

Meine Freundin lebt auf dem Land da zieht
Zweimal am Tag die eine Schafherde am Fenster vorbei
Einmal am Abend die zweite, die Wohnung ist freundlich
Der Mann klug gütig fast schön die
Kinder gesund alles in Ordnung, morgens
Singt meine Freundin wenn sie das Baby badet
Schenkt allen Äpfel, die Sonne
Sieht sehr schön aus in den Trauerweiden
Dahlien haben sich aufgeblättert Staub rieselt sacht in sie
Wenn Trecker die bleichen Rüben fabrikwärts fahren
Ich schlafe sehr gut dort am Rande der Welt
Nachdem
Ich sie gierig machte auf Schiffe und Meere

Return

My friend lives in the country where
Twice a day a herd of sheep goes by the window
A second herd passes in the evening, her apartment's pleasing
Her husband clever kind almost beautiful the
Children healthy all is well, in the morning
My friend sings as she bathes the baby
Gives everyone apples, the sun
Looks wonderful in the weeping willows
Dahlias have opened up dust flutters into them
When tractors take the pale turnips off to the factory
I sleep contented there at the edge of the world
After
Making her long for ships and seas

Engel

Ich sah einen er kam im Taxi der Vordersitz
War flachgelegt so hatte er Platz
Man hob ihn heraus vor dem kleinen Fischgeschäft
Geleitete ihn in einen geschorenen Garten
Da stand er ernst in der Luft überragte
Die ihn stützten seine Augen erreichte nichts
Die Kleider waren verblaßt Goldreste
Überzogen die Brust er war ohne Flügel
Seine Führer lehnten ihn an einen Karren
Blockierten zuvor die Räder damit er
Nicht ins Gleiten käme sich etwa zerschlüge
Ich sah seine Hände sie waren leer
Hatten wohl vorher den Ölzweig getragen oder
Ein Saitenspiel jahrhundertelang
Jetzt war er taxiert unterwegs auf Wohnungssuche
Erst ins Antiquitätengeschäft was wird aus ihm wer
Braucht schon einen Engel der so groß ist
Er füllt eine Küche stände
Wo besser ein Kühlschrank steht oder der Tisch mit
Der Brotschneidemaschine, der Ausweg für ihn
Wäre ein Kindergarten wenn der ihn beherbergte
Wer wüchse nicht gern mit einem Engel auf

Angels

I saw one he came in a taxi the front seat
Was laid flat to make space for him
They lifted him out in front of the little fish shop
Escorted him into a close-cropped garden
He hovered there solemnly in the air over-towering
Those supporting him his gaze fixed on nothing
His clothes were faded gold vestiges
Coated his chest he was wingless
His guides leaned him up against a cart
Whose wheels they had jammed so that
It wouldn't roll off and crash perhaps
I saw his hands they were empty
Had of course held the olive branch earlier
Or for hundreds of years a stringed instrument
Now he was being taxied about hunting for a flat
First stop the antique shop what will become of him
Who on earth needs an angel who's so large
He fills a kitchen and would occupy space
Better used for a fridge or the table with
The bread slicer on it, the alternative
Would be for a playschool to take him in
Who wouldn't like to grow up with an angel

Bilder

Meine Mutter treibt die Ziege
Niemals hat sie die besessen
Übers grüne Blätterdach
Meines Vaters Uhren schlagen
Nacheinander in der Nacht
Der Bruder ist sehr jung gestorben
Seine Blumen wachsen wild
Seit er sie nicht mehr zählt
Meine Stadt ging auf in Flammen
Menschen liefen in die Kirchen
Und verbrannten mit den Bildern
Ich sah sie liegen ohne Furcht
Ich war klein und las die Ähren
Auf vom Acker in der Frühe
Wenn der Mittag heiß vorbei war
Übte ich mich auf dem Rad
Oder saß in unserm Garten
Wand Jasmin zu runden Kränzen
Legte sie ertrunknen Vögeln
Auf die hübschen steilen Hügel
Klirrt die Gartentür jetzt bellt
Dieser zugelaufne Hund
Ach der Vater meiner Mutter
Treibt mich aus den vollen Bäumen
Und ich stehe vor den Beeten
Wo die kalten Astern gleißen
Trete ihre späten Köpfe
Unter meine Nachkriegsschuhe

Images

My mother drives the goat
She never ever owned
Over the green leaf canopy
At night my father's clocks
Strike one after the other
His brother died very young
His flowers have been growing wild
Ever since he stopped counting them
My town went up in flames
People ran into the churches
And burned along with the paintings
I saw them lying unafraid
I was small and gleaned the corn
From the field in the morning
When the midday heat passed
I practised riding my bike
Or sat about in our garden
Wound jasmine into wreaths
And set them out for drowned birds
On the lovely steep mounds
The garden gate clanks now
This strayed dog is barking
Oh my mother's father
Drives me from the full-leafed trees
And I stand before the beds
Where the cold asters gleam
Trample their late heads
Beneath my post-war shoes

Ich bin sehr sanft

Ich bin sehr sanft nenn
Mich Kamille
Meine Finger sind zärtlich baun
Kirchen in deiner Hand meine Nägel
Flügelschuppen von Engeln liebkosen ich bin
Der Sommer der Herbst selbst der Winter im Frühling
Möchte ich bei dir sein du
Zeigst mir das Land wir gehn
Von See zu See da braucht es
Ein langes glückliches Leben
Die Fische sind zwei
Die Vögel baun Nester wir
Stehn auf demselben Blatt

I am very gentle

I am very gentle call
Me Chamomile
My fingers are tender build
Churches in your hand my nails
Wing scales of angels caress I'm
Summer autumn even winter in springtime
I'd like to be with you you can
Show me the countryside we will travel
From lake to lake we'll need
A long happy life for that
The fish are paired
The birds are making nests we're
On the same page

From

Zaubersprüche

(Incantations)

Schwarze Bohnen

Nachmittags nehme ich ein Buch in die Hand
Nachmittags lege ich ein Buch aus der Hand
Nachmittags fällt mir ein es gibt Krieg
Nachmittags vergesse ich jedweden Krieg
Nachmittags mahle ich Kaffee
Nachmittags setze ich den zermahlenen Kaffee
Rückwärts zusammen schöne
Schwarze Bohnen
Nachmittags ziehe ich mich aus mich an
Erst schminke dann wasche ich mich
Singe bin stumm

Black beans

In the afternoon I pick up a book
In the afternoon I put a book down
In the afternoon it enters my head there is war
In the afternoon I forget each and every war
In the afternoon I grind coffee
In the afternoon I put the ground coffee
Back together again gorgeous
Black beans
In the afternoon I take off my clothes put them on
Apply make-up first then wash
Sing don't say a thing

Die Nacht streckt ihre Finger aus

Die Nacht streckt ihre Finger aus
Sie findet mich in meinem Haus
Sie setzt sich unter meinen Tisch
Sie kriecht wird groß sie windet sich

Und der Rauch schwimmt durch den Raum
Wächst zu einem schönen Baum
Den ich leicht zerstören kann –
Ich rauch einen neuen, dann

Zähl ich alle meine lieben
Freunde an den Fingern ab
Es sind zu viele Finger, die ich hab
Zu wenig Freunde sind geblieben

Streckt die Nacht die Finger aus
Findet sie mich in meinem Haus
Rauch schwimmt durch den leeren Raum
Wächst zu einem Baum

Der war vollbelaubt mit Worten
Worten, die alsbald verdorrten
Schiffchen schwimmen durch die Zweige
Die ich heut nicht mehr besteige

The night extends its fingers

The night extends its fingers
It finds me at home
It sits down under my table
It crawls it grows it blows

And smoke floats through the room
Grows into a pretty bush
I can easily ruin –
I light another cigarette, then

Count all my dear friends
On my fingers
I have too many fingers
Too few friends are left

If the night extends its fingers
It will find me at home
Smoke floating through the empty room
Growing into a bush

Which was laden with words
Words that withered straight away
Ships swim through the branches
I no longer climb these days

Mai

Auf dem Dach der großen Klinik
Sitzen feiertags die Kranken
In gestreiften Bademänteln
Legen Finger auf die Wunden
Rauchen eine Zigarette

Auf der Erde ist das Gras grün
Gelbe Blumen sind darin
Und die weißen Küchenfrauen
Ziehen Karren mit Kartoffeln
Fleisch Kompott Gemüse. Wieder

Kommt ein Krankenwagen
Mit der Fahne und der schrillen
Stimme die um Eile schreit
Ach ich seh dich blütenblaß
Neben deinem Auto liegen

May

On holidays the patients sit
On the big clinic's roof
In striped dressing gowns
Fingering their wounds
Smoking cigarettes

On the ground the grass is green
With yellow flowers in between
And the white kitchen ladies
Pull carts with potatoes
Meat, vegetables, compote. Yet

Another ambulance
With its flag and shrill voice
Wailing to go faster
Oh I see you petal-pale
Lying there beside your car

Die Engel

Der Himmel auf tönernen Füßen
Wir fahren darunter in kleinen Autos
Die Brücken
Fangen ihn ab eine Zeit lang
Wird er blau sein, Vögel
Und Nacht und Tag und manchmal
Ein Nordlicht in fremden Breiten
Einer wird, in verwirrenden Farben, ihn sehen
Wenn ihm gut oder nicht ist und der Mond und die Sonne
Hineingeschossene Löcher
Werden kühlen wärmen bis dann
Die letzte Stunde gekommen ist
Und die Engel mit eiskalten Augen
Die großen Blätter auf denen Geschichte verzeichnet ist
Einrollen ein neues
Licht anzünden

The angels

The sky on clay feet
We travel beneath it in small cars
The bridges
Block it for a while
It will be blue, birds
And night and day and sometimes
A northern light in foreign climes
Someone, in dazzling colours, will see it
Whether he's feeling well or not and the moon and sun
Penetrated holes
Will cool warm up until
The final hour has come
And angels with ice-cold eyes
Furl the large leaves on which history's
Recorded turn on
A new light

Mittelmeer

Der alte Dichter war da
Er erzählte vom Thunfischfang wenn
Die übermanngroßen Tiere
Ins Netz getrieben werden wie sie toben
Der Leitfisch bringt alle und die Schuppen
Glänzen wie rostfreier Stahl
Er aß Kirschkuchen
Hatte die Welt im Blick
Sicher erinnert er sich
Wie die Nacht da schmeckte
Seine Augen warn blauer als sonst
Und ich hörte die Fischer singen
Die dem Thun Haken in die Köpfe schlagen
Eine Handbreit vom Auge
Einmal sagte er haben die großen Tiere
Einen Mann fast aus dem Boot gehoben
Die Boote waren tiefschwarz
Und acht Meter lang

Mediterranean

The old poet was there
Telling tales of the tuna catch
Of how the creatures larger than a man
Go mad when driven into the net
The pilot fish delivers them and their scales
Shine like stainless steel
He was eating cherry cake
Held the world in his gaze
He can certainly remember
How the night tasted then
His eyes were bluer than usual
And I heard the fishermen sing
As they drilled hooks into tuna heads
A hand's width from the eyes
Once he said the large creatures
Almost hauled a man from the boat
The boats were a deep shade of black
And eight metres long

Lithographie

Die Pforte war gebogen und wir kamen durch
Nachdem wir einen Mann mit weißen Haaren
Der noch nicht alt war, Geld bezahlten und er gab
Ein vogelstimmig Fräulein uns zur Seite

Die Alte flog voraus, nahm Weg durch Steine
Die uns wie Zähne eines Tiers erschienen
Wir wähnten einzugehn ins Maul des Wales
Der Jonas zu verschlingen einst geschickt war

Es waren Steine zum Gedächtnis alter Juden
Gewaltlos starben sie in dieser Stadt
Und sanken schichtweis in die Erde, weil der Platz
Gering war und von Häusern eingeschlossen

Nur große Bäume kamen auf an dieser Stelle
Sie standen blattlos in den dünnen Himmel
Doch schienen sie nicht schlecht im Saft zu sein

Der eine wuchs dem Rabbi aus dem Kopf
Bis seine Wurzeln ihn verlassen mußten
Weil nichts mehr war, die Zweige zu ernähren

Das Vogelfräulein klappte mit dem Schnabel
Sie stopfte uns noch die Jahre in die Ohren
Bevor sie aufflog im Geäst verschwand

Wir laufen Zickzack durch die schwarzen Male
Damit wir draußen gegenwärtig sind
Dies ist kein Ort, wir waren auf Papier
Vorher, auf Stein, gezeichnet und geätzt.

Lithography

The gate was arched and we passed through
After paying a man with white hair
Who wasn't yet old, and he assigned
A spinster with a bird's voice as our guide

The old woman flew on ahead, making her way through stones
That seemed to us like animal teeth
We imagined we were entering the maw of the whale
Once sent to swallow Jonah

The stones were in memory of old Jews
Who died peacefully in this town
And sank in layers into the ground,
Since the square was small and surrounded by houses

Only large trees grew here
Standing bare in the thin air
Yet did not seem to lack sap

One grew out of the rabbi's head
Till its roots had to desert him
Because there was nothing left to nourish its branches

The bird lady banged with her beak
She crammed more years into our ears
Before she flew up disappearing among the branches

We zigzag through the black memorials
To be out in the open
This is not a place, before we were
On paper, on stone, drawn and etched.

Der Droste würde ich gern Wasser reichen

Der Droste würde ich gern Wasser reichen
In alte Spiegel mit ihr sehen, Vögel
Nennen, wir richten unsre Brillen
Auf Felder und Holunderbüsche, gehn
Glucksend übers Moor, der Kiebitz balzt
Ach, würd ich sagen, Ihr Lewin –
Schnaubt nicht schon ein Pferd?

Die Locke etwas leichter – und wir laufen
Den Kiesweg, ich die Spätgeborne
Hätte mit Skandalen aufgewartet – am Spinett
Das kostbar in der Halle steht
Spielen wir vierhändig Reiterlieder oder
Das Verbotne von Villon
Der Mond geht auf – wir sind allein

Der Gärtner zeigt uns Angelwerfen
Bis Lewin in seiner Kutsche ankommt
Schenkt uns Zeitungsfahnen, Schnäpse
Gießen wir in unsre Kehlen, lesen
Beide lieben wir den Kühnen, seine Augen
Sind wie grüne Schattenteiche, wir verstehen
Uns jetzt gründlich auf das Handwerk Fischen

I would gladly hold a candle to Droste

I would gladly hold a candle to Droste
Look into old mirrors along with her, identify
Birds, we'd direct our eyeglasses
At fields and elder bushes, go
Chortling over the moor, the lapwing courts
Och, I would say, your Levin –
Isn't that a horse snorting already?

The tress somewhat gentler – and we'd take
The gravel walk, I the late-born
Would have entertained with scandals – on the spinet
That stands luxuriously in the hall
We'd play duets knight songs or
The forbidden one by Villon
The moon goes up – we are alone

The gardener shows us how to cast a line
Until Levin arrives in his coach
Gives us newspaper banners, we pour
Schnapps down our throats, we both
Read and love the bold one, his eyes
Are like green shadow ponds, you and I
Are dab hands now at the art of fishing

Rufformel

Phöbus rotkrachende Wolkenwand
Schwimm
Ihm unters Lid vermenge dich
Mit meinen Haaren
Binden ihn daß er nicht weiß
Ob Montag ob Freitag ist und
Welches Jahrhundert ob er Ovid
Gelesen oder gesehen hat ob ich
Sein Löffel seine Frau bin oder
Nur so ein Wolkentier
Quer übern Himmel

Summoning spell

Apollo red crashing wall cloud
Swim
Under his eyelids mingle in
With my hair
Bind him so he doesn't know
If it's Monday or Friday and
Which century whether he has
Read or seen Ovid if I am
His lug his wife
Or just a cloud-animal
Clear across the sky

Ich

Meine Haarspitzen schwimmmen im Rotwein, mein Herz
Sprang – ein Ei im kochenden Wasser – urplötzlich
Auf und es fiel, sprang wieder, ich dachte
Wo du nun wärest, da flogen die Schwäne dieses
Und auch des anderen Spreearms schnell übern Himmel.
Das Morgenrot, das dezemberliche, Bote
Vielleicht frühen Schnees, hüllte sie ein und die Hälse
Verlockung, sich zu verknoten, sie stießen
Fast mit der Kirche zusammen. Ich stand
Auf eigenen Füßen, Proleten unter den Gliedern, ich hätte
Mir gern einen Bärn aufgeladen ein Zopf aufgebunden
Ein Pulverfaß aufm Feuer gehabt.

Me

The tips of my hair are swimming in red wine, my heart
Jumped – an egg in boiling water – all of a sudden
And it fell, jumped again, I thought
Wherever you now were the swans of this
And the Spree's other arm were flying fast across the sky.
The red dawn, December's, a sign
Perhaps of early snow, enveloped them enticing
Their necks to intertwine, so they collided
With the church almost. I stood
On my own two feet, proles among the limbs, I would
Gladly have carried a bear worn a pigtail
Had a powderkeg on the fire.

From

Rückenwind

(Tailwind)

Tilia cordata

Langsam nach Jahren geh ich
Vom Sein des Hunds in das der Katze.
Ich will davon nicht reden, nur so viel:
Ich wollte für ihn was verzeichnen
Ein poetisches Bild: das ging mir
Plötzlich wie Honig ein: die Linden
Fingen zu blühen an und ich hatte gesehn
Daß die Bäume Ähnlichkeit haben mit Mädchen
Blondhaarigen, die Strähnen rötlich
Leichthin gelockt. Die großen Mädchen
Man sieht in die
Halbkurz geschnittenen Locken von unten. Ne Spur
Von Ohrringen, baumelnd, Kugeln
Hochverschlossene Knospen inmitten
Sich verschleudernder spreizender Blüten – ich dachte bloß
Nun sehe ich schon Mädchen? Doch mich
Betraf das nicht, ich sah seine Augen.

Tilia cordata

Slowly years later I am changing
From a dog into a cat.
I don't want to talk about it, except to say:
I wanted to record something for him
A poetic picture: that suddenly
Entered me like honey: the lime trees
Were beginning to blossom and I'd seen
That the trees resemble girls
Blonde-haired ones, with reddish strands
Gently curled. Big girls whose mid-length curls
You look up into from below. A hint
Of earrings, dangling, globes
Tightly closed buds amidst
Extravagant open blooms – I just thought
Am I in fact seeing girls? But this
Did not bother me, I saw his eyes.

Die Luft riecht schon nach Schnee

Die Luft riecht schon nach Schnee, mein Geliebter
Trägt langes Haar, ach der Winter, der Winter der uns
Eng zusammenwirft steht vor der Tür, kommt
Mit dem Windhundgespann. Eisblumen
Streut er ans Fenster, die Kohlen glühen im Herd, und
Du Schönster Schneeweißer legst mir einen Kopf in den Schoß
Ich sage das ist
Der Schlitten der nicht mehr hält, Schnee fällt uns
Mitten ins Herz, er glüht
Auf den Aschekübeln im Hof Darling flüstert die Amsel

The air already smells like snow

The air already smells like snow, my love
Is wearing his hair long, oh the winter, the winter which
Throws us close together's at the door, it's coming
With the wind hound team. It's sprinkling
Ice flowers on the window, coals glow on the stove, and
You most handsome snow-white man lay your head in my lap
I say that is
The sleigh that no longer stops, snow falls
Straight through our hearts, it glows
On the ash bins in the yard Darling whispers the blackbird

Rückenwind

Wie er mich jagt, sein Schrei
Mich vorwärts trägt fünfundzwanzig
Windsbräute in der Sekunde
Den ganzen Tag, am Abend, und in die Nacht.
Ich komme zur Welt ich singe vor ihm
Jubel und Lachen: Die Finger
Des himmlischen Kinds auf meiner Schulter.

Und hör ich die Stimme des Einen
Von großer Schönheit
Dreht sich der Gegenwind, ich fliege
Und immer zu ihm
Klopfendesherz wie das Haus schwankt

Tailwind

How he chases me, his cry
Carries me forward twenty-five
Tempests per second
All day, in the evening, and into the night.
I come into the world I sing to him
Exultation and laughter: the fingers
Of the heavenly child on my shoulder.
And when I hear the voice
Of the most beautiful one
The headwind turns, I fly
And always to him
My throbbing heart how the house birls

Der Meropsvogel

Der große
Sehr schöne Meropsvogel
Fliegt schon im Frühjahr kaum zeigt sich ein Blatt
Davon in den Süden wo Schatten
Höchst senkrecht fallen der Stein
Warm wie meine Augen-Blicke auf ihn

So hab ich gelernt; groß ist er stark schön wie
Ein Mensch und weiß man von ihm
Hört die Sehnsucht nicht auf. Er fliegt doch er sieht
Fliegend zurück, er entfernt sich, nähert sich trotzdem.
Über die Augen. Das Blut. Zum Herzen. O schöne Sage! Ein
Springen von Stein zu Stein; Hoffnung
Wo Raum und Zeit sich
Zwischen uns legen. Und kommt er wieder? Er kommt.
Herangesehnt zurückgewünscht erwartet erwartet
So blickt er fliegend zurück, mich nicht an.
Er naht er entfernt sich.

The bee-eater

In spring
When hardly a leaf is visible
The large very beautiful bee-eater
Already heads south where shadows fall
Most vertically the stone warm
As my glances at him

This much I've learned: he is big strong and handsome
As a man and if you know of him
Your longing never ends. He flies but looks back
As he flies, withdraws, yet advances nonetheless.
Through the eyes. The blood. To the heart. Oh wonderful
                                                legend! A
Hopping from stone to stone; Hope
Where space and time
Interpose between us. And will he come again? He will.
Longed for wished back awaited awaited
Flying he looks back, not at me.
He advances he moves away.

Das Fenster

Die vielen Himmel über
Sehr flachem Land! Im ersten
Fliegen die Elstern, im zweiten

Hochfahrende Wolken. Der dritte
Für Lerchen. Im vierten
Sah ich ein Flugzeug stehn.

Aus dem fünften funkelt der Stern.
Die toten Schmetterlinge auf den Dielen.
Bevor es zerfällt, verkauft man ein Haus.

The window

The many skies above
Very flat land! In the first
Fly magpies, in the second

High-travelling clouds. The third
Is for larks. In the fourth
I saw an aeroplane hang.

From the fifth twinkles a star.
Dead butterflies on the floorboards.
You sell a house before it falls apart.

Allein

Die alten Frauen vor roten Häusern
Roten Hortensien verkrüppelten Bäumen
Brachten mir Tee. Würdevoll
Trugen sie die Tabletts zurück, bezogen
Horch- und Beobachtungsposten
Hinter Schnickschnackschnörkel-Gardinen.

Alone

The old women in front of red homes
Red hydrangeas stunted trees
Brought me tea. With dignity
They carried back the trays, took up
Listening and observation posts
Behind twirly-frilly-tacky curtains.

Der Milan

Donner; die roten Flammen
Machen viel Schönheit. Die nadligen Bäume
Fliegen am ganzen Körper. Ein wüster Vogel
Ausgebreitet im Wind und noch arglos
Segelt in Lüften. Hat er dich
Im südlichen Auge, im nördlichen mich?
Wie wir zerrissen sind, und ganz
Nur in des Vogels Kopf. *Warum*
Bin ich dein Diener nicht ich könnte
Dann bei dir sein. In diesem elektrischen Sommer
Denkt keiner an sich und die Sonne
In tausend Spiegeln ist ein furchtbarer Anblick allein.

The kite

Thunder: the red flames
Create a lot of beauty. The needle-shaped
Trees fly with their entire bodies: a wild bird
Splayed on the wind and still trusting
Sails through the air. Has he got you
In his southern eye, me in the northern one?
How we are torn, and whole
Only in the bird's head. *Oh why*
Am I not your servant I
Could be with you then. In this electric summer
No one is thinking of himself and the sun
In a thousand mirrors is a terrible sight alone.

Der Süden

Wenn es nach mir ginge, ich säße den Tag
Angelehnt auf dem Faulbett, den Himmel
Vergleichend und Bilder vor Augen.
Über die Straße flattert ein Landhund;
Die alten Papierfabriken! Das grüne reine Wasser.
Mein Arm drinnen, der andere
Zugereicht. Höchstens vier Grad die Sorgue.
Petrarca kommt mit Laura den Weg uns entgegen
Auf einem Maultier. Beide über siebzig und Laura
Rauchte Zigarrn. Der Maler Klapper holt aus einem Schuhkarton
Fünfundzwanzig angefangene Bilder. Ein Ockertagebau
Ein Schwemmsystem um den Farbstoff zu fangen – alles
Unterm Mont Ventoux eines Tags im September, der
Währt schon ein Jahr

The south

If I had my way I would spend the day
Lying in my easy chair, comparing
The sky with pictures in my mind.
A country dog flits across the street;
The old paper mills! The green pure water.
My one arm in it, the other reaching
Over. The Sorgue at most four degrees.
Petrarca comes towards us on the path with Laura
On a donkey. Both over seventy and Laura
Used to smoke cigars. Klapper the artist takes out of a shoebox
Twenty-five paintings he has started. An ochre open-cast mine
An alluvial system to catch the dye with – all that
Under Mont Vertoux one day in September, that's
Already lasted a year

Einäugig

Wie Ölbäume schimmern die Weiden
Blaugrün und zitternd, die Pappeln
Ahmen Zypressen nach (dunkler
Dunkler! Vertieft eure Schatten!). Der Wind
Übt Fall und Flug seines Bruders Mistral.

One-eyed

Like olive trees the willows are glimmering
Blue-green and quivering, the poplars
Are imitating cypresses (darker
Darker! Deepen your shadows!). The wind
Is practising the dip and soar of its brother the mistral.

Raubvogel

Raubvogel süß ist die Luft
So kreiste ich nie über Menschen und Bäumen
So stürz ich nicht noch einmal durch die Sonne
Und zieh was ich raubte ins Licht
Und flieg davon durch den Sommer!

Bird of prey

Bird of prey sweet is the air
I never wheeled like this before above people and trees
I'll never again plunge through the sun
Like this and pull what I've plundered into the light
And fly off through the summer!

From

Drachensteigen
(Kite Flying)

Allereirauh

Aber am schönsten: mit dir
Oder ohne dich
Über die Boulevards laufen nichts im Gepäck
Als Rosinenbrot, Wein und Tabak
Die Leute der Länder festhalten
Im Auge und später
Sprechen davon, den Himmel beschreiben den Schnee
Du kommst mit dem Westwind und ich
Aus dem Norden, wir tragen
Das alles zusammen, die winzigen Pferde
Die senkrechten Palmen, die Sterne, Kaffeemaschinen
Nachmittags halb nach vier, wenn die Glocke
Im Käfig schaukelt und schreit

All-kinds-of-fur

But nicest of all: with you
Or without you
Strolling down the boulevards nothing in my rucksack
But raisin bread, wine and tobacco
Watching people from other countries
And talking about it all afterwards,
Describing the sky the snow
You come with the west wind
And I from the north, we bring
All that together, the tiny horses
The vertical palms, the stars, coffee machines
In the afternoon at half three, when the bell
In the cage swings and screams

Der Rest des Fadens

Drachensteigen. Spiel
Für große Ebnen ohne Baum und Wasser. Im offenen Himmel
Steigt auf
Der Stern aus Papier, unhaltbar
Ins Licht gerissen, höher, aus allen Augen
Und weiter, weiter

Uns gehört der Rest des Fadens, und daß wir dich kannten.

What's left of the string

Kite flying. A game
For large plains without trees and water: In the open sky
The paper
Star rises, unstoppably
Drawn to the light, higher, out of sight
And farther, farther on

Ours is what's left of the string, and having known you.

The Last of November

Erst in die Wechselstuben am Zoo, die letzten
Silbernen Pferdchen aus allen Manteltaschen.
Umtausch – ein toller Kurs, es blieb noch was übrig.
Der Wind der Wind, unheimliches Kind
Blies uns im schönen Kabriolett
Hin an den Reichstag.
Schneebeeren rieselten, kleines Getier
Raschelte an dem furchtbaren Ort.
Das ist die Mauer. Stellenweis grüner Kalk.
Türmchen und Aussichtspodeste hüben und drüben.
Alles registrieren sagt er, wie Hemingway
Auf dem Rückzug in Spanien das stinkende Pferd.
Wir fuhren und flogen
Dreimal um den frischvergoldeten Engel, trafen
Unsere toten Dichter in ihren Wagen (die flogen
Schneller und schöner als wir)

The last of November

First stop the bureau de change at the Zoo, the last
Little silver horses out of all our coat pockets.
Exchange – a fantastic rate, something was left over.
The wind the wind, sinister kid
Blew us in our nice convertible
Over towards the Reichstag.
Snow-berries trickled, small animals
Rustled at that terrible spot.
That's the Wall. Green limestone in parts.
Turrets and lookout posts on this side and that.
Record everything he says, like Hemingway
Did the stinking horse during the retreat in Spain.
We drove and flew
Three times round the freshly gilded angel, met
Our dead poets in their chariots (flying
Faster and finer than us)

Jedes Blatt

Ich sage dir was ich sehe manchmal
Jedes Blatt einzeln am Baum oder
Aufm Kies kleine Sicheln oder wie das
Weitergeht mit mir: kurze Aufenthalte
Alles wieder zusammenpacken und fort

Each leaf

I tell you what I sometimes see
Each leaf singly on the tree or
Little sickles in among the stones or
How things will go for me: short stop-overs
Packing everything up again and off

Unglück läßt grüßen

Seit er fort ist fallen Palmen
Um gehen Bomben los, ich bin
Von Moskitos verbeult oder schneide
Mir halbe Finger ab, es kommt noch
Schnee im August

Disaster sends its regards

Since he's been gone palms have been toppling
Over bombs exploding, I've been
Battered by mosquitoes or have cut
My fingers half off, it's even
Going to snow in August

Villa M.

O und immer
Läuft dieser
Schimmernde Hund
Durchs wilde Gras wirft die Pfoten
Unmengen Gänseblümchen gerupfte Federn und schließlich
Die allwissenden dumpfen Zypressen

Villa M.

Oh and always
This lustrous
Dog runs
Though the wild grass throwing its paws
Masses of daisies plucked feathers and last of all
The omniscient dull cypresses

Flaute

Es regnet nicht und es schneit nicht
Weder Sonne noch Wind, alles
Wie unter Wasser. Die Häuser
Völlig verschlossen und taub.

Lull

It's not raining and it isn't snowing
Neither sun nor wind, everything
As if under water. The homes
Totally closed-up and deaf.

Das schöne Tal

Die Landschaft ist groß und voller Bewegung. Über den Bergen
Wird Licht ausgegossen, schwarze Wolken
Verzehrn es und Blitze
Bespringen sich kalt kracht der Donner.

Das ist die Sintflut. Alles in einer Glocke.
Wir fließen naß im Auto zu Tal.
Die Tiere die Kröten Salamander Geccos
Flattern ins Handschuhfach. Er legt mir
Die Hand in den Schoß.

The lovely valley

The landscape is large and full of movement. Light's being poured
Over the mountains, black clouds
Are devouring it and lightning bolts
Are mounting one another the thunder's crashing cold.

This is the flood. Everything in a bell.
We're floating wet in our car down to the valley.
The animals the toads lizards geckos
Are fluttering into the glovebox. He lays
His hand in my lap.

Verloren

Das Bett hat sich
Weit von der Wand entfernt, die Bewegung
Ist groß, in zwei Wochen
Steht es auf der Piazza Navona oder
Wir segeln Mund an Mund durch die Berge wenn nur
Die Leintücher fest sind

Lost

The bed has wandered
Far from the wall, the movement
Is enormous, in two weeks
It will stand on the Piazza Navona or
We'll be sailing mouth to mouth through the mountains if only
The sheets hold

Gennaio

Boreas brüllt, zerfetzt wohl die Bäume.
Die Amseln sprechen nicht mehr.
Der Gärtner schwebt über geschnittenen Hecken, notiert
Die abgestürzten Orangen.

Wir zwischen weißen Tüchern
Knöchlein an Knöchlein.

Gennaio

Boreas is bawling, ripping up trees it seems.
The blackbirds are no longer talking.
The gardener's hovering over chopped-off hedgerows, logging
The oranges that have fallen.

We're between white sheets
Lying bone to bone.

From

Erdreich
(Earth)

Bären

Niedergehende kleine Gebirge
Klopften unterm Tioga-Paß
Die einzelnen Bären raus aus den Höhlen
Sie standen still in der ernsten Luft
Kristallbeschlagen und wirklich verdrießlich
Der schwarze der eisgefesselte See
Ertrug unsern Fuß, viel stumme Vögel
Stoben aus den geköpften Tannen, die niedren Wolken
Gerieten so in Bewegung zerteilten sich Schnee
Fällt dir auf den Mund das weiße Gestöber
Will dich mir wegführn, und gleich.
Ich liebe dich komm ich bin doch
Inmitten der Bären ich rede wahrhaftig
Und wenn mir diese mächtigen Tiere
So durch den Kopf gehn
Müssen sie dagestanden haben
Anfang Dezember die Pfoten im Wind

Bears

Disintegrating small mountain ranges
Knocked the solitary bears
Beneath the Tioga Pass out of their caves
They stood quietly in the solemn air
Studded with crystals and really irked
The black the icebound lake
Held our weight, many silent birds
Flew up from the beheaded firs, the low clouds
Got so tumultuous they broke up
Snow falls onto your mouth the white drifts
Want to lead you away from me, immediately.
I love you come I am after all
In among the bears speaking honestly
And if these powerful creatures
Are now flitting through my head like this
They must have been standing there
Early in December their paws in the wind

Chinesisches Hotel

Jeden Morgen bevor wir
Ins Castro-Viertel
Oder zum Cliffhouse
Und den Seehunden aufbrechen
Husten zweihundert Chinesen
Hinter papierdünnen Wänden
Der krachende rasselnde
Berstende Lärm
Das Röcheln und Keuchen
Jaspen und Ächzen
Das Räuspern
Beunruhigt mich
Und ein schreckliches Schleifen
Schlurfen und Schleppen
Hebt an vor der Tür
Der lange Marsch
Der vierhundert Füße
Kleines hinkendes Gleiten
Großmütter auf gewickelten Zehen
Trippeln und Tappen
In die Etagenküche
Der Korridor wirft
Die Stimmen zurück
Alles Soprane sie rufen
Überstürzende Silben
Geschimpfe vielleicht
Und Seufzen und Murmeln
Zischen und Wispern
Trifft unser Ohr
Jetzt hat das große Volk
Endlich die Küche erreicht
Es schiebt scheppernde Töpfe
Klappernde schurrende Pfannen
Mit gewölbten Böden aufs Feuer
Das Fett prasselt und schreit
Exotischer Duft ohnegleichen
Haifischflossen und Entenfüße

Chinese hotel

Every morning before we
Set out for
The Castro quarter
Or the Cliff House and the seals
Two hundred Chinese cough
Behind paper-thin walls
The crashing rattling
Banging noise
The groaning and gasping
Moaning and panting
The clearing of throats
Disturbs me
And a terrible dragging
Shuffling and hauling
Starts in front of the door
The long march
Of four hundred feet
Small hobbling steps
Of grandmothers on bound toes
Toddling and tripping
Into the kitchen on our floor
The corridor throws
Back their voices
All sopranos they are shouting
In hurried syllables
Curses perhaps
And sighing and moaning
Mumbling and murmuring
Greet our ears
Now the large crowd
Has finally reached the kitchen
And is pushing clattering pots
Shuffling and clanking woks
Onto the stove
The fat crackles and screams
Unequalled exotic smells
Of shark fins duck feet

Quillt mir durch den Luftschacht
Federn fliegen am Fenster vorüber
Wir flüchten in die stürzenden
Sich aufbäumenden Straßen
Der zärtlichen Stadt
Kaufen im Drugstore
Eishampoo meine Haare
Sind eichhörnchengrau
Redwoodrot
Und in der kleinen Halle
Des Hotels Sam Wong
Sitzen die verstaubten
Gerade noch lebenden
Alten Chinesen wie immer
Schwatzend im Rollstuhl
Wenn wir über alle Brücken
Zurückgekehrt sind.

Waft up through the air duct
Feathers fly past the window
We flee into the teeming
Rearing streets
Of the tender city
Buy egg shampoo
In the chemist's my hair
Is squirrel grey
Redwood red
And in the small lobby
Of the Sam Wong hotel
The fusty barely still living
Old Chinese are sitting chattering
As always in their wheelchairs
After we've come back
Across all the bridges.

Landwege

Wir konnten uns nicht erinnern
An welcher Stelle das Wasser
Hin in den Untergrund ging und seit wann
Wir dieser Stromleitung folgten.
Die Blumen waren wohl lange verdorrt
Wie graue Esel lagen die Berge
Fünf Horizonte entfernt und wir rollten
In glitzernder bunter Luft
Auf einen irdenen endlosen Teller.

Country roads

We could not recall
At which spot the water
Went underground and how long
We'd been following the electric cables.
The flowers had withered long ago
The mountains lay like grey donkeys
Five horizons away and we were rolling
In glittering multi-coloured air
Onto an earthen edgeless plate.

Bäume

Ich bin den Bäumen nachgerannt im anderen Erdteil
Den Namen wollte ich wissen ihre Verwandtschaft
Seit wann sie das Land so bevölkern die Wurzeln
Treppenstufen hervor aus dem Boden reißen
Ihre Stämme sind nur zu dritt zu umspannen
Die Rinde ist tiefgefurcht schwarz ihre Äste
Gleichen dem Leib der Pythonschlange sie tragen
Gefingerte ledrige Blätter blaue Vögel in Trauben
Die Taxifahrer sagten das wären hier so die Bäume
In einer Bibliothek von fünfzehn Etagen
Waren in den Straßen und Häusern langer Regale
Herrliche Nachschlagwerke über Gott und die Welt
Seit Jahren untergekommen Enzyklopädien Atlanten
Viel Welthistorien Schauspielerführer Glossare
Alles aus dem Leben der Schmetterlinge
Aber die knorrigen Dinger von vor der Tür
Die Mitglieder weitreichender Tunnelalleen
Konnte ich im botanischen Viertel nicht finden
Auf jeder Party fing ich wieder an von den Bäumen
Die Leute reichten mir Wasser und Brot erzählten
Stundenlang von verschiedenen Möglichkeiten Gewächse
Während der Nacht feierlich zu beleuchten
Meine Erkundungen waren ein Schlag ins Wasser
Die Bäume standen nach wie vor namenlos da
Bis ich aufgeben und abreisen mußte
Wenn ich an sie denke grüne Gestalten geschieht es
Mit einem merkwürdigen Gefühl der Leere.

Trees

I chased after trees in another part of the world
I wanted to know their name their family
How long they had populated the land
Their roots displacing paving in the ground
It takes three people to embrace their trunks
The bark is deeply furrowed black their branches
Are like a python's body they have
Fingered leather leaves clusters of blue birds
The taxi drivers said that was the way trees were here
In a fifteen-storey library
The streets and houses of long shelves held
Magnificent reference works on all the world and his wife
Ancient encyclopaedias atlases
Many world histories guides to actors glossaries
Everything you'd want to know about butterflies
But the gnarled objects on the doorstep
Which formed extensive tunnelled avenues
Could not be found in the botany quarter
At parties I went on about the trees
People gave me bread and water and talked to me for hours
About how to light up plants nocturnally
My enquiries led nowhere
The trees still had no name
When I had to pack up and leave
Whenever I think of them those green shapes
It's with a strange empty feeling.

Fluchtpunkt

Heine ging zu Fuß durchs Gebirge
Er vertrödelte sich in Häusern, auf Plätzen
Und brauchte zwei Wochen für eine Strecke
Die wir in einem Tag durchgefahrn wären
Unsere Reisen führen von einem Land
Gleich in das nächste von Einzelheiten
Können wir uns nicht aufhalten lassen
Uns zwingen die eignen Maschinen
Ohne Verweilen weiterzurasen Expeditionen
Ins Innre der Menschen sind uns versagt
Die Schutthalden Irrgärten schönen Gefilde
Bleiben unerforscht und verborgen
Die Kellner brauchen unsere Zeitung nicht
Ihre Nachrichten sind aus dem Fernsehn
Es gibt verschiedene Autos eine Art Menschen
Alles ist austauschbar wo wir auch sind.

Vanishing point

Heine went walking through the mountains
He loitered in houses, in squares
And took two weeks to cover a stretch
We would leave behind us in a day
Our travels lead from one country
Straight into the next we can't let
Details hold us up.
Compelled by our inner engines
To race on without delay we miss out
On expeditions into people's hearts
The rubble tips labyrinths lovely fields
Remain unexplored and concealed
The waiters don't need our paper
Their news comes from the TV
There are different types of cars one kind of people
Everything's replaceable wherever we are.

Die Übung

Eines Morgens vor einem Jahr
Die jungen Linden
Die von hieraus schnurgrade
Durchs Brandenburger Tor
Hin zu den großen ziehn blühten
Ich kam aus dem Zigarettenladen
Die kleinen Revolver die Gaspistolen
Glänzten zwischen den Pfeifen
An diesem gewöhnlichen Morgen
Der so hübsch war
Weil nichts besondres geschah
Die Katze im Wollgeschäft
Spielte mit Wolle
Der Maßschneider unterhielt sich am Fenster
Das Mädchen vom Antiquitätenladen
Hängte ein Brautkleid
Von neunzehnhundertfünf an die Tür
Der Briefmarkenhändler träumte
Von der blauen Mauritius
Der persische Teppichverkäufer
Fuhr mit dem Staubsauger
Zwischen den bunten Beeten
Seines Zaubergartens hin und her
An der Tankstelle gegenüber
Wurden Rosen gepflanzt
Der Goldschmied und Uhrmachermeister
Hinter der Lampe hatte die Lupe
Ins Auge geklemmt und sein sehr treuer Hund
Wedelte mit dem coupierten Schwanz
An diesem freundlichen hellen Morgen
Wollte ich auf der Straße
Äpfel und Kirschen kaufen
Hatte die Hand ausgestreckt als plötzlich
Ein Trupp erhitzter Soldaten
Bis an die Zähne bewaffnet
Im Laufschritt hereinbrach

The exercise

One morning a year ago
The young lime trees
Which pull dead straight from here
Through the Brandenburg Gate
Down to the large ones were in bloom
I came out of the tobacconist's
The little revolvers the gas pistols
Were shining in among the pipes
On this ordinary morning
Which was so nice because
Nothing special was going on
The cat in the wool shop
Was playing with wool
The bespoke tailor chatting at his window
The girl from the antique shop
Was hanging a wedding dress
From 1904 on the door
The stamp dealer was dreaming
Of the Blue Mauritius
The Persian carpet seller
Was passing his vacuum cleaner
Backwards and forwards
Among the colourful beds
Of his magic garden
At the petrol station opposite
They were planting roses
The goldsmith and watchmaker
Behind his lamp had a magnifying glass
Clamped to his eye and his very faithful dog
Was wagging his stump of a tail
On this bright pleasant morning
I was about to buy apples
And cherries on the street
I'd stretched out my hand when suddenly
A squad of het-up soldiers
Armed to the teeth
Broke into a run

Sie sangen ein seltsames schnelles Lied
Stießen Schreie hervor wie beim Töten
Der Commander hatte die lauteste Stimme
Der Letzte lief auf verwundeten Füßen
Die Passanten erstarrten
Schreckliche ausführliche Gedanken
Verschüttete Bilder
Flogen durch ihre Köpfe
Das gehetzte Zufußrennen
Beeindruckte mehr als eine Panzerparade
Der Spuk zog vorüber das Frösteln
Die Leute wischten sich was
Wie Spinnweben von den Augen
Das angehaltene Leben ging weiter
Die Autos waren wieder zu hören
Der Schneider ließ die Maschine sausen
Das Brautkleid sah ein bißchen
Nach Ferntrauung aus
Kinder stürzten aus der Schule
Schrien mit Spatzenstimmen.

They were singing a strange quick song
Shrieking as if they were killing someone
The Commander was the loudest of them all
The one at the end had injured feet
The passers-by froze
Terrible detailed thoughts
Suppressed images
Flew through their heads
The harried running made
A greater impression than a tank parade
The ghost passed the shivering
People wiped something
Like spiders' webs from their eyes
Life started back up
Cars could be heard again
The tailor let his machine rip
The wedding dress looked a little
Like marriage by proxy
Kids ran out of school
Screeching with sparrows' voices.

Naturschutzgebiet

Die weltstädtischen Kaninchen
Hüpfen sich aus auf dem Potsdamer Platz
Wie soll ich angesichts dieser Wiesen
Glauben was mir mein Großvater sagte
Hier war der Nabel der Welt
Als er in jungen Jahren mit seinem Adler
Ein schönes Mädchen chauffierte.
Durch das verschwundene Hotel
Fliegen die Mauersegler
Die Nebel steigen
Aus wunderbaren Wiesen und Sträuchern
Kaum sperrt man den Menschen den Zugang
Tut die Natur das ihre durchwächst
Noch das Pflaster die Straßenbahnschienen.

Nature reserve

The cosmopolitan rabbits
Are hopping about on the Potsdamer Platz
In view of these open fields how can
I believe what my grandfather told me
That this was the hub of the world
When he as a young man would chauffeur
A beautiful girl in his Adler.
Swifts are flying
Through the vanished hotel
The mist is rising
From wonderful meadows and shrubs
Hardly has man been barred
Than nature does its part grows back
Even through cobbles and tram tracks.

Erdreich

Nachrichten aus dem Leben der Raupen
Der Kuckuck stottert und die gebackenen Beete
Zerreißen sich wenn ich Gießkannen schleppe
Die mir überantworteten Gewächse verlausten Gemüse
Hilflos betrachte, als ich vor Jahren
In meines Vaters Garten ging
Gab es die siebfachen Plagen
Höllisches Ungeziefer nicht und der Boden
Tat noch das Seine, der hier
Ist ein Aussteiger niederträchtig und faul
Ihn muß man bitten den Dung
Vorn und Hinten einblasen sonst bringt er
Nicht maln Pfifferling vor was müssen die Menschen
Das Erdreich beleidigt haben, mir erscheint
Siebenundzwanzig Rosenstöcke zu retten
Ein versprengter Engel den gelben Kanister
Über die stockfleckigen Flügel geschnallt
Der himmlische Daumen im Gummihandschuh
Senkt das Ventil und es riecht
Für Stunden nach bitteren Mandeln.

Earth

News from the life of caterpillars
The cuckoo is stammering and the baked beds
Crack up when I drag watering cans
Look helplessly at the louse-ridden vegetables
That have been placed in my charge, years ago
When I went into my father's garden
The seven-fold plagues hellish pests
Did not exist and the earth
Still did its bit, this here
Is a drop-out vile and lazy
You have to beg it blow in
Dung in all directions or it
Doesn't even bring forth a chanterelle,
How people must have offended the earth,
To save twenty-seven rose trees
A scattered angel comes to me
A yellow canister strapped to its mouldy wings
The heavenly thumb in the rubber glove
Presses down on the valve
And it smells for hours of bitter almonds.

Spektakel

Die Elstern auf dem steilen Dach
Unverständlich was sie bezwecken
Mühn sich für nichts und wieder nichts
Langschwänzige schlurfende schreitende
Dauernd verwandelte tragische komische Vögel
Die sich am Ende verbeugen die Krähen
Sind blaß vor so viel Gerissenheit Kunst.

Spectacle

The magpies on the steep roof
Whose purpose can't be understood
Toil for nothing at all
Long-tailed scuffling strutting
Constantly transformed tragic comic birds
That bow when they come to the end the crows
Blanch at so much craftiness art.

Die Berührung

Das Rauschen der Bäume die
Schwankenden Sträucher Stimmen der Tiere
Lange leuchtende helle Blumen
Selbst das Netz der Spinne am Fenster
Alles hat die Nacht weggenommen
Wir stecken einsam in den Gehäusen
Nirgendwo ist noch ein Licht zu sehn
Und die Scheibe spiegelt die Lampe
Zwiefach zurück mir durch den Leib
Es ist nicht sicher, träte ich
Gleich aus der Tür alles wiederzufinden
Wie es im Licht stand, und streckte ich
Die Hand nach dem rauhen
Armdicken Stamm der Sonnenblume aus
Ich griffe ins Leere oder berührte
Schmales Handgelenk einer vergeblichen
Sonnenblumenesserin, Schalen und Kerne
Fallen ihr auf die Schuhe über die
Blaue Jacke mit dem buckligen P

The touch

The rustle of the trees the
Swaying shrubs animals' voices
Long shining bright flowers
Even the spider's web at the window
The night's removed everything
We're secluded in our shells
Nowhere is there a light in sight
And the windowpane's reflecting the lamp
Back through my body twice
It's not certain if I now
Stepped outside to find everything
As it was in the light, and stretched
Out my hand for the rough
Sunflower stem thick as an arm
If I'd reach into emptiness or touch
The thin wrist of a clumsy
Sunflower eater, husks and seeds
Spilling onto her shoes down the
Blue jacket with the hunchbacked P

Selektion

Welche Unordnung die Rosenblätter
Sind aus den Angeln gefallen der Wind
Blies sie ums Haus auf die Gemüsebeete.
Streng getrennt wachsen hier in den Gärten
Magen- und Augenpflanzen, der Schönheit
Bleibt ein einziges Beet
Während den ausgerichteten Reihen
Früher Kartoffeln Möhren Endivien Kohl
Ein Exerzierplatz eingeräumt wird.

Die Wirrnis des Gartens verwirrt
Auch den Gärtner, jetzt muß
Durchgegriffen werden angetreten Salat
Richtet euch Teltower Rüben Rapunzel
Auf den Abfallhaufen Franzosenkraut
Wucherblume fälsche Kamille und Quecke
Es ist verboten die nackten Füße
Wieder ins Erdreich zu stecken.

Selektion

What disorder the rose petals
Have come unhinged the wind
Has blown them round the house onto the vegetable patch.
In gardens here stomach- and eye-plants
Grow strictly apart, and only
One bed is reserved for beauty
While the lined-up rows
Of new potatoes carrots endives cabbages
Have been granted a parade ground.

The muddle of the garden befuddles
Even the gardener, now drastic measures
Must be taken fall in at attention lettuce
Right dress Teltow turnips corn salad
To the rubbish heap gallant soldier
Chrysanthemums feverfew and witchgrass
It is forbidden ever again
To stick bare feet in the earth.

Beginn der Zerstörung

Unbegehbar von Mooren umschlossen
Niemals hat ein Mensch ein vierfüßiges Tier
Diese verhexte lockende Wiese betreten
Die Rinder der schwarzen Bäume, Säulen
Des Himmels, berührt, die vielstimmigen Vögel
Auffahren sehen aus geschüttelten Blättern
Wunderschöne Vögel mit Hauben, Spechte
In sehr großer Menge, blaugefiederte Tauben
Und noch die Kühe, stumpfsinniges Vieh
Benachbarten Graslands versuchen mitunter
Den Saum zu erreichen, es heißt sie mißachten
Den eigenen Zaun und zerreißen
Sich Brust und Kopfschild versinken.
Die rostbraunen Wasser betrügerischen Moose
Werfen uns alle zurück. Wir sehen
Die Wiese vom Tau beglänzt Tag und Nacht
Ihre Blumen, die nie eine irdische Hand
Fällte, Sterne, weitverzweigter Halme
Schwebende Kronen, und sind
Von aller Freude abgeschnitten durch
Unser Wünschen, wir in gewöhnlichen
Kuhweiden stehend voll Sehnsucht.

The beginning of destruction

Impassable surrounded by fens
No person no four-legged animal has ever
Entered this tempting meadow
Touched the barks of the black trees, pillars
Of the sky, or seen the many-voiced birds
Start up from shaken leaves
Wonderful birds with caps, large numbers
Of woodpeckers, blue-feathered doves
And the cows as well, mindless cattle
From neighbouring pasture attempt now and then
To reach the edge, it is said they flout
Their own fence and rip
Their chests and their head shields sink.
The rust-brown waters of deceptive mosses
Cast us all back. We see
The meadow shine with dew day and night
Its flowers, which no earthly hand
Has gathered, stars, swaying crowns of
Ramified blades of grass, and we are
Cut off from all joy
By desire, standing in common
Pastures full of longing.

Verwilderung

Meingott es sind doch Farne
Grüne Pfauen und Strauße
Die im Rosenbeet Platz genommen haben
Sind sie im Sturm geflogen
Oder dem alten Bahndamm kurzerhand
Von Schwelle zu Schwelle gesprungen

Wildness

Heavens they really are ferns
Green peacocks and ostriches
That have seated themselves in the rose bed
Did they fly here in the storm
Or just plain hop from sleeper to sleeper
Along the old railway embankment

Zunehmende Kälte

Der Winter brach zeitig herein
Schon im November zeigten
Die Thermometer arktische Zahlen
Trotzdem schneite es ununterbrochen
Bald sahen nur noch die Dächer
Einzelne Kronen sehr hoher Bäume
Hervor aus dem flimmernden Weiß.

Maulwürfen gleich gruben die Menschen
Gänge vom Haus in die Scheunen
Die Klagen hörten nicht auf
Welche Arbeit die Türen zu öffnen
Wie an die Futtermieten gelangen
Und Wasser für die Tiere erwärmen
Bis die Hochspannungsmaste
Beim letzten Schneesturm zusammenfielen.

Jetzt verendete Vieh in so großer Anzahl
Daß die Abdecker und Knochenmühlen
Ihrer Arbeit nicht nachkommen konnten
Die steifgefrornen Kadaver im freien Feld
Täglich aufgetürmt werden mußten
Von Brettern und Steinen gehalten
Und mit Schaudern dachten die Bauern
An plötzliche mildere Tage.

Als ich eingewickelt in doppelte Tücher
Mit Fellstiefeln Pelzhandschuhn
Brennspiritus holen ging sah ich

Eine Katze aufrecht erfroren
Tot wie sie ging und stand
Die grünen Augen funkelten noch
Über den Feldweg zum Dorf.

Increasing cold

The winter started early
Already in November the thermometers
Were showing Arctic temperatures
Despite this it snowed non-stop
Soon only the roofs a few tops
Of very high trees were visible
In the shimmering white.

People like moles dug passages
From their homes to the barns
There were never-ending complaints
What a job opening the gates
How to reach the mangers
And heat up water for the animals
Until the pylons collapsed
In the last snowstorm.

Now animals were dying in such large numbers
That the knackers and bone grinders
Couldn't keep up with the work
The frozen stiff carcasses in the open field
Had to be stacked up daily
Held in place by planks and stones
And the farmers thought with a shudder
Of suddenly milder days.

When I swathed in double layers
In pelt boots fur gloves
Went to fetch meths I saw

A cat frozen upright
Struck dead mid-stride
Its green eyes were still sparkling
Over the track to the village.

Erdrauch

Und zu verschiedenen Zeiten geschieht es
Daß wir sehr glücklich über
Irgend ein Ding eine Nachricht
Den neuen Geliebten das Kind
Umhergehen können da freut uns
Die eintönigste Arbeit da kochen wir
Wunderbare Gerichte putzen die Fenster
Und singen dabei küssen
Die eben aufgesprungene Blüte
Am Strauch vor der Tür reden
Zu Unbekannten über die Straße
Und beachten die Sonne nicht
Den leichten tanzenden Schnee
Es ist alles bekannt und vertraut
So wird es immer sein glauben wir
Und noch die furchtbaren Bilder
In den Fernsehgeräten bestärken uns
Wenigstens hier wird es so bleiben wir stapeln
Die Zeitungen die uns ruhig schlafen lassen
Sorgfältig auf bis sie abgeholt werden
Wir sind ganz lebendig hüpfen und springen
In den möblierten Wohnungen des Todes

Terrestrial smoke

And on occasion it happens
That we walk about ecstatic
About something or other a piece of news
Our new lover our kid
Then the most tedious chore
Pleases us we sing as we cook
Wonderful dishes clean the windows
And kiss the newly formed blooms
On the bush by the door
Speak to strangers across the road
And ignore the sun
The light dancing snow
All this is familiar and known
And even the terrible images
On our TV screens confirm for us
That here at least things will stay the same
We stack with care till they're collected
The papers that let us sleep in peace
Completely alive we jump and leap
In our furnished flats of death

From

Katzenleben

(Cat Lives)

Sanfter Schrecken

Der Himmel erinnerte mich
An weiße Veilchen die in der Mitte
Des Kelchs eine Spur Rosa zeigen
Sehr viele weiße Veilchen und ein paar blaue
Wieder war alles gründlich verwandelt
Geschliffene Klarheit vielfache Linien
Die Häuser sehr nah und ihr Innres
Lag durchsichtig vor mir ich sah
Bis in die Seele des Bäckers, die letzten
Erschrockenen Mücken wärmten die Füße
An meinem Fenster, jeder Halm
War geschärft frisch angespitzt und ich zählte
Nebenäste vierundzwanzigster Ordnung
Die Welt bestand aus Einzelheiten
Es war genau zu unterscheiden
Welches übriggebliebene Blatt
Um ein weniges vor oder hinter
Anderem leis sich bewegte.

Gentle fright

The sky reminded me
Of white violets with a touch
Of pink in the centre of their cups
A great many white violets and a few blue ones
Everything was thoroughly changed again
Heightened clarity multiple lines
The houses very near and their interiors
Lay bare before me I could see
Straight into the baker's soul, the last
Frightened flies were warming their feet
On my window, every stalk
Was sharpened freshly pointed and I counted
Branches of the twenty-fourth order
The world consisted of details
It could clearly be perceived
Which remaining leaf
Moved quietly slightly behind
Or in front of the other.

Schnee

Wie sich vor unseren geübten Augen
Alles verwandelt das Dorf fliegt
Um Jahrhunderte rückwärts im Schnee
Es bedarf dazu einiger Krähen
Kopfweiden am Weg altmodische Hunde
Liebe und Treue gelten du ziehst mich
Über Gräben trägst mein gestohlenes
Bündelchen Holz in den Abend
Lebendiger Rauch hüllt die Dächer.

Snow

How everything changes
Before our practised eyes
Transported by crows the village flies
Back centuries in snow
Roadside pollard willows old-fashioned hounds
Love and loyalty hold good you
Drag me over ditches carry my pilfered
Bundle of wood into the evening
Vivid smoke enshrouds the roofs.

Dritter Wurf

Die jungen Katzen stürzen regelmäßig
Eh sie die Leitersprossen erreichen
Vom Heuboden ab auf das Pflaster des Kuhstalls.
Nach dem ersten Todesfall wirft der Bauer
Stroh unter die Luke die grauen Geschwister
Übernehmen am mütterlichen Bauch
Die Zitze des Wegbereiters ihre Chancen
Zu überleben sind sprunghaft gestiegen.

Third litter

Before they reach the ladder rungs
The young cats regularly tumble
Headlong down from the loft
Onto the cowshed's cobbled floor.
After the first fatal fall
The farmer tosses straw beneath the hatch
The grey siblings now share the forerunner's teat
Their chance of survival is rapidly increased.

Reglos

Der Tag kommt an aus den Wäldern
Unsichtbar es schneit in die Grenzen
Von gestern und heute ich kann
Auf der Erde nichts unterscheiden
Alles ist ununterscheidbar und gleich
Die Spuren der Wölfe der Lämmer
Die erfrorenen Hasen deckt Schnee
Er legt sich auf umgeblasene Bäume
Die lebenden will er ersticken
Er läßt die Bäche verschwinden
Moore und Teiche Felder alles ist
Gleich tot und begraben im Dämmerlicht
Sinkender drehender Schnee die Augen
Verwirren sich schwarze Flocken
Asche fällt nicht steigt auf oder der Himmel
Läßt sich herab weil die Geschöpfe sich ducken
Atemlos reglos die Stille wesenlos mondlos
Es ist nicht hell und wird nicht dunkel
Niemand geht auf den Feldern die Felder
Totenfelder wachsen hirtenlos stündlich
Der Schneefall dauert lang wie mein Leben
Ich habe den Namen der Ortschaft vergessen
Und die Straßen aufgehobenen Plätze
Wir befinden uns kurz nach dem Frieden
Wir können uns nicht erinnern was
Alles geschah das ausgelöschte Bewußtsein
Menschenleer gedankenlos kein Licht
Kein Schatten gepunktete Bilder und nur
Die Kraft sich nicht zu bewegen.

Motionless

The day emerges from the forest
It snows invisibly into the borders
Between yesterday and today
I can't distinguish anything on the ground
Everything's exactly the same
Snow covers the tracks of wolves
Of lambs and frozen hares
It lays itself on blown-down trees
Wants to suffocate the living
It makes brooks disappear
Fens and ponds fields everything
Equally dead and buried in the gloom
Falling twirling snow the eyes
Become confused black flakes
Ash doesn't fall but rises or the sky
Lowers itself because the creatures are crouching
Breathless motionless the silence incorporeal moonless
It's not light and it doesn't get dark
No one walks in the fields the fields
Fields of the dead grow shepherdless by the hour
The snowfall lasts as long as my life
I've forgotten the name of the town
And the street names superseded squares
It's just after the peace
We cannot recall what all
Happened the obliterated consciousness
Empty of people bereft of thought
No light no shadow dotted pictures
And only the strength to stand still.

Das Gehäuse

Es ist dunkel im Haus Wassergardinen
Fließen vor den Fenstern bis zum Dreikönigstag
Wird die Weihnachtstanne geduldet
Auf den Lichtstümpfen zucken die Flammen
Wind drückt das dichtgefaltete Wasser
Eng an die Scheiben es blühen die
Zwiebelgewächse weiß blau und rosa
Die Dunkelheit fällt aus den Ecken
Schleicht über die Schwellen verkriecht sich
In sich selbst und unter die Betten
Die Stille quillt aus Truhen und Schränken
Und in der warmen greifbaren Düsternis
Die ich durchstoße die sich hinter mir schließt
Die wie violetter Samt herumhängt sich
Aufrollt und bläht in jedem Topf sitzt
Traktiert der den ich liebe plötzlich den Flügel
Mit zu Tränen rührenden Stücken
Die Katze kippelt auf ihrem Lieblingsstuhl
Die Dachrinnen laufen über an den
Vorbestimmten Stellen die betrunkene Seele
Des Zimmermanns klappert im Dachstuhl.

The housing

It's dark in the house water curtains
Are flowing down in front of the windows we put up with
The Christmas tree until Epiphany
Flames flicker on the candle stumps
Wind presses the tightly pleated water
Up close against the window panes bulbous plants
Bloom white blue and pink
Darkness tumbles out of every corner
Creeps across the thresholds crawls
Into itself and under the beds
Silence wells up from cupboards and chests
And in the warm tangible gloom
Which closes behind me after I pass through
That hangs around like purple velvet
Rolls itself up expands and sits in every pot
The one I love suddenly mauls the grand piano
With pieces that move me to tears
The cat tilts on her favourite chair
The gutters overflow where they should
The carpenter's drunken soul clatters about
In the trusses of the roof.

Anfang des Tages

Die Treibhausblumen leuchten in der
Dämmrigen Diele, hinterm Rücken des Hauses
Feiert die morgendliche sehr frische Sonne
Märzorgien die Alte ist wohl durch den
Winter gelangt schmückt sich mit Glaube
Liebe Hoffnung die Krone stachelt Vögel
Zu Lärm an sie schleppen Halme stürzen
Und steigen und Katzen schweben nach
Der Maulwurf beginnt sein einsames Handwerk
Alte Frauen gehen in Gärten sie zählen
Blumen vertreiben Hühner glätten Mulden
Sind sehr zufrieden über der Erde wenn sie
Der Männer gedenken die schon am Rande
Des Dorfes angelangt sind in Särgen.

Daybreak

The hothouse flowers are glowing
In the gloomy hall, behind the back of the house
The very fresh morning sun's performing
March orgies for the old woman's come
Through the winter adorning her crown
With Faith Love Hope she goads birds
To make a racket dragging stalks they dive
And soar and cats hover after them
The mole starts his lonesome craft
Old women go out into gardens and count
Flowers hector chickens fill in ditches
Are very happy above ground when they recall
The men who've already reached the limits
Of the village in coffins.

Die Ausschweifung

Keinen Hut nur die Hennahaare aufm Kopf
Unter Mittag leidenschaftlich den Pfeilen
Der Sonne ausgesetzt in strahlenden Beeten
Ohne Schatten von Haus und Baum
Kniend verwünschtes Unkraut ausreißen
Wunderbare sich selbst verschlingende
Wiedergebärende Kreise lackrote Räder
Drehn sich im Kopf Schwärze und
Schwindel brechende Dämme
Hundegebell am Rand des Bewußtseins
Der Kuckuck aus einer anderen Welt
Die Reihen schlingern im Beet Borretsch
Und Pimpernell tanzt durch die Melde
Nur die Hände sind ganz lebendig
Sinken und steigen
Wie ein Paar Schwalben.

Excess

No hat only hennaed hair on my head
Exposed with ardour to the arrows
Of the midday sun kneeling in radiant beds
Without the shade of house or tree
To pull up cursed weeds
Amazing circles that consume themselves
Then begin again red lacquered wheels
Turn in my head blackness and
Dizziness bursting dams
Barking at the edge of consciousness
The cuckoo from another realm
The rows roll in the borage bed
And pimpernel dances through the pigweed
Only my hands are fully alive
Falling and rising
Like a pair of swallows.

Musikstunde

Seine Mutter lehrt meine Gartenfinger
Über die Tasten zu springen
Das Pianoforte hat einen Riß
Bellt daß dem Sahnekännchen
Widerstandslos der Henkel abbricht.

Ich wende mich sanften Dingen zu
Wie der Hausherr im Rollstuhl
Die Gartentreppe hinabfährt
Über die grauen Schleifenblumen
Und keine Spur hinterläßt.

Music lesson

His mother teaches my green fingers
To leap across the keys
The cracked piano blasts the handle
Off the jug for the cream
And meets no resistance.

I turn to gentle things
As the host glides his wheelchair
Down the garden steps
Over the grey candytufts
And leaves no trace.

Raben

Die Bäume in diesen windzerblasenen
Das Land überrollenden Himmeln
Sind höher als die zusammengeduckten
Gluckenähnlichen Kirchen, und Wolken
Durchfliegen die Kronen die Vögel
Steigen von Ast zu Ast kohlschwarze Raben
Flattern den heidnischen Göttern
Hin auf die Schultern und krächzen
Den Alten die Ohren voll alle Sterblichen
Werden verpfiffen schlappe Seelen
Über den Wurzeln und ohne Flügel.

Crows

The trees in these wind-ravaged skies
Rolling across the land are higher
Than the churches crouched together
Like a clutch of broody hens, and clouds
Fly through their crowns the birds
Rise from branch to branch coal-black crows
Flap onto pagan gods' shoulders
And caw their old ears full
Grassing on mortals limp souls
Without wings above the roots.

Zugeflogene Rose

Ersprießlicher ist der Umgang mit Pflanzen
Sie kehren wieder oder es herrscht
Gewißheit daß sie in einem einzigen Sommer
Ihr grünes Leben verschleudern Unfälle
Sind leicht zu ertragen die abgemähte
Einst zugeflogene Rose
Wird durch den Kürbis ersetzt und die
Bäume sind fast unschlagbar
Dauerhafter als der eigene Leib
Braucht der Liebhaber sich nicht
Um ihr Fortkommen sorgen der Tod
Hinsinkender sturmgebrochener Riesen
Ist ein erhabener schmerzloser Anblick.

The rose that blew in

Consorting with plants is more rewarding
They either return or will most certainly squander
Their green life in a single summer
Mishaps can be easily borne the mowed-down
Rose that once blew in
Gets replaced by a pumpkin
And the trees are hard to top
More lasting than one's own body
No lover need worry
About them carrying on
The death of toppling
Storm-ravaged giants
Is an exalted painless sight.

Katzenleben

Aber die Dichter lieben die Katzen
Die nicht kontrollierbaren sanften
Freien die den Novemberregen
Auf seidenen Sesseln oder in Lumpen
Verschlafen verträumen stumm
Antwort geben sich schütteln und
Weiterleben hinter dem Jägerzaun
Wenn die besessenen Nachbarn
Immer noch Autonummern notieren
Der Überwachte in seinen vier Wänden
Längst die Grenzen hinter sich ließ.

Cat lives

Poets love cats of course
The gentle free who cannot be controlled
Who sleep and dream November rain away
On silk chairs or in rags speak back
Without saying a word shake themselves
And get on with their lives
Behind the hunter's fence
While his possessed neighbours
Are still noting down licence plates
The one being observed in his four walls
Has long left the borders behind.

Die Verdammung

Weil ihm zu sterben verwehrt war
Angekettet dem heimischen Felsen der Blick
Auf die ziehenden Wolken gerichtet und immer
Allein die Bilder im Kopf stimmlos
Von Rufen Anrufen Verdammen
Das Leben fristen war nicht zu bedenken
Göttliche Hinterlist nährte ihn so gewöhnte
Er sich langsam ins Schicksal nach Jahren
Sah er den Adler gern wenn er nahte und sprach
Stotternd mit ihm bei der Verrichtung

Oder mit entzündeten Augen verrenktem Hals
Weil der Flügelschlag ausblieb die niederen Wälder
Aufschub ihm angedeihn ließen um Tage
Harrte er des einzigen Wesens und glaubte
In der Leere des Winds der glühenden Sonne
Wenn der Fittiche Dunkel fürn Augenblick
Erquickung schenkte geborgen zu sein
Liebte den Folterer dichtete Tugend ihm an

Als die Ketten zerfielen der Gott
Müde geworden an ihn noch zu denken
Der Adler weiterhin flog weil kein
Auftrag ihn innezuhalten erreichte
Gelang es ihm nicht sich erheben den
Furchtbaren Ort für immer verlassen
In alle Ewigkeit hält er am Mittag
Ausschau nach seinem Beschatter.

Damnation

Because he was denied death
Chained to his native cliff his gaze
Directed at drifting clouds and always
Alone the images in his head voiceless
From shouting cursing calling
With no need to think about scraping a living
Since godly skulduggery nourished him
Slowly he got used to his fate and after some years
He was pleased to see the eagle when it appeared
And stuttered at it as it did its work

Or when the low woods held it up
And he did not hear the beat of wings for days
He waited for the only being his eyes inflamed
With a twisted neck and in the emptiness of wind
And blistering sun believed himself protected
When the wings' shadow granted him a brief reprieve
Loved his torturer imputed virtue to him

When the chains fell away when the god
Had tired of thinking of him
The eagle continued to fly because
It never got an order to stop
He never managed to get up
And leave the terrible place forever
For all eternity at midday
He keeps a lookout for his tail.

Querfeldein

Wir sprachen unterirdisch erst durch die
Heide Steingräber heulten im Wind dann
Mecklenburg Brandenburg durch und es war
Ein herrlicher Morgen Veilchenwolken
Über Chausseen hochfliegende Schwalben
Wir hörten die Kühe über den Kabeln
Unsere unvergeßlichen treuen Stimmen die
Kiebitze ordentlich schrein die Sicherheit
War mit von der Partie Elke sagte
Wie mühsam es ist Tag und Nacht
Ein Atemloch offen zu halten ich sah sie
Im lichtlosen Wald als es grenzenlos schneite
In durchgelaufenen Turnschuhen stehn.

Cross country

We spoke at first underground through the heather
Stone tombs howled in the wind then
Through Mecklenburg Brandenburg and it was
A glorious morning violet clouds
Above the country roads high-flying swallows
We heard the cows over the wires
Our unforgettable loyal voices
The kibitzes duly squealing Security
Was listening in Elke said
How hard it is day and night
To keep a breathing space open I saw her
Standing in the dark wood as snow erased the borders
In worn-out trainers.

Bäume

Früher sollen sie
Wälder gebildet haben und Vögel
Auch Libellen genannt kleine
Huhnähnliche Wesen die zu
Singen vermochten schauten herab.

Trees

It is said that in times gone by
They formed forests and that birds
Also called dragonflies
Small creatures like singing hens
Looked down from them.

From

Schneewärme
(Snow Warmth)

Demetrius

Wie ein Pirol lebe ich
In den Kronen der Bäume
Berühre den Boden nicht
Liebe die Wolken aber der
Falsche Kaiser er wimmert
Nach meiner Seele.

Gezinkt war seine Rede jetzt
Ist er am Ende ich aber
Lebe in den Baum-
Kronen ewig
Lache über den
Falschen Dimitri das greinende
Holz ohne blühenden Zweig.

Demetrius

I live like an oriole
In the tops of trees
Do not touch the ground
Love the clouds but the
False Kaiser's whimpering
After my soul.

His speech was well controlled
Now he's reached the end but I
Will live in the tree-
Tops forever
Laughing at the
False Dimitri the whimpering
Wood without a blooming twig.

Freyas Katzen

Über dem Meer geht jetzt der
Abendstern auf und Bjarni sagt
Es sei die Göttin der Liebe:
Unglänzt und gnadenlos
Lächelt sie aus dem Wagen
Gezogen von weißen
Schnurrenden Katzen.

Die schönen Tiere. Geputzt
Gilt ihre Jagd jetzt den Männern.
Die Himmelstiere sind versehn
Mit Mädchenaugen und bringen
Lust und alles Elend darnach.
Die Kratzer sagt Bjarni von denen
Bleiben für immer.

Freya's cats

The evening star's now rising
Above the sea and Bjarni says
It's the goddess of love:
Bathed in light and merciless
She smiles from her chariot
Pulled by white purring cats.

The lovely animals. Scrubbed up
They're now hunting for men.
The celestial creatures are equipped
With girls' eyes and bring
Pleasure and all sorts of misery in its wake.
Their scratches Bjarni says never fade.

Eisrosen

In diesem Winter blühten die Rosen einfach weiter.
Triefende Nebellaken dämpften jedes Geräusch.
Die Dohlen knarrten stundenlang auf unserer Insel
Sie waren nicht imstande den Ort zu verlassen.
Der grüne Deich eine Zunge auf der ich stand früh
Am Morgen kam aus dem Nichts und führte auch wieder
Hinein. Ein paar Meter Gras in der Luft dahinter
Reißt alles ab und ich bin es zufrieden.
Welche Überraschung so unvermutet am
Ende zu sein friedlich in all
Dem wässrigen Weiß in lockere Laken geschlagen.

Ice roses

This winter the roses simply carried on blooming.
Dripping wet sheets of fog dampened all sound.
Jackdaws rasped for hours on our island
They could not leave the place.
The green dyke a tongue on which I stood early
In the morning came out of the ether and led back in
Again. A few metres of grass in the air behind it
Rips everything apart and I am pleased.
What a surprise to be so unexpected
In the end at peace in all the watery white
Wrapped in loose sheets.

Begrenztes Licht

Der Nebel hat alles
In seine Totenwäsche geschlagen das Wasser
Bricht durch Fenster und Türen es treibt
Meine Schätze davon die Deckel aufgeklappt
Als wäre es Plunder das Nebelhorn
Spielt seine tragische Weise
Eine Weile schwimmen Gäbelchen Erstausgaben
Die selbstgefällige Dielenuhr mit einem
Zeitgefühl das schon lange nicht mehr
Intakt ist und die geputzten Blumenzwiebeln
Allen voran die Morgen- und Abendgrüße
Unserer Hände sieben Jahre unter dem
Dachfirst gestapelt sie sinken
Ins schwarze dampfende Wasser.
Es ist schön über den Dingen stehn
Wenn die Flut ansteigt.
Dieser trübe Nebel von Jahren.
All diese Jahre voll Nebel.

Restricted light

The fog's enveloped everything
In its death-wash the water is
Breaking through windows and doors driving
My treasures off the lids flipped
Up as if it were all junk the foghorn
Plays its tragic song
For a while swim tiny forks first editions
The smug hall clock whose sense of time
Has long been out of whack
And the shiny plant bulbs
Above all else the morning and evening greetings
Of our hands stacked for seven years
Under the ridge of the roof they're sinking
Into the black reeky water.
It is nice to stand above things
When the flood begins.
This bleak fog of years.
All these years full of fog.

Eichbäume

Als die Bewohner sich zerstreuten die Mehrheit
Der Gefiederten aufbrach in andere Breiten das Laub
Klirrend nach starken Frösten herabfiel
Wurde sichtbar der Leib des Windharfenwalds:
Anmutige Wirbelsäulen Zweige für jede Gebärde
Widersetzlich knarrende splitternde Schönheit.

Oak trees

When the inhabitants scattered the majority
Of feathered ones set off for other latitudes
And the foliage crisp after heavy frosts fell off
The heart of the wind harp forest could be seen:
Graceful spinal columns branches for every gesture
Contrasting rasping splintering beauty.

Schwarze Schuhe

Das Meer hat bodenlose Täler und Krater
Der Himmel Kuppeln und Gipfel darüber.
Die Falten des grünen Meers im Dezember
Lappen über die Barkasse samt Personal
Den angezündeten Christbaum. Der Lotse
War natürlich kein Lotse und vierhundert
Schwarze Schuhe werden an Land gespült.
Es lassen sich später wieder Paare
Zusammenstellen am Ufer der Hallig
Eiliges Strandgut kurz vor dem Fest
Dies und das seit Menschengedenken.
Es ist ein leichtes Leben hier am
Rande des Wassers wenn nicht die
Ölpest den Anblick verdirbt Vogelkadaver
Ein- und ausgeatmet vom grünen so
Grünen Meer im Dezember.

Black shoes

The sea has bottomless valleys and craters
The sky above it domes and summits.
The folds of the green December sea
Lap over the launch and its crew
The illuminated Christmas tree. The pilot
Was of course no pilot and four hundred
Black shoes are washed up onto land
Pairs are later matched up again
On the Hallig shoreline
Urgent flotsam and jetsam
Shortly before the holiday
This and that in living memory.
It's an easy life here
At the edge of the water if only
Oil pollution doesn't spoil the view and birds' carcasses
Aren't breathed in and out by the green
So green December sea.

Wintermusik

Bin einmal eine rote Füchsin ge-
Wesen mit hohen Sprüngen
Holte ich mir was ich wollte.

Grau bin ich jetzt grauer Regen.
Ich kam bis nach Grönland
In meinem Herzen.

An der Küste leuchtet ein Stein
Darauf steht: Keiner kehrt wieder.
Der Stein verkürzt mir das Leben.

Die vier Enden der Welt
Sind voller Leid. Liebe
Ist wie das Brechen des Rückgrats.

Winter music

I was once a red fox
With high jumps
I got what I wanted.

Now I am grey grey rain.
I made it as far as Greenland
In my heart.

On the coast shines a stone
On which is written: no one returns.
The stone shortens my life.

The four corners of the world
Are full of sorrow. Love
Is like breaking your spine.

Entfernung

Das halbe Leben vom Leben der Katzen
Spielt in hohen Träumen sich ab sie gehen
Weite Strecken im Schlaf oder fliegen
In blauen Wolken geflügelten Dingen nach.

Ist man hier weiß man von dort nicht mehr
Viel. Was ich erlebt habe ist mir entfallen.
Eigentlich gab es nichts zu verstehn.
O dieses mondsüchtige Leben von Katzen.
Wie Hasenbrot die Vergangenheit nun.

Distance

Half the life of the lives of cats
Is set in high-flying dreams in sleep
They cover vast tracts or fly
Through blue clouds after feathered creatures.

When you're here you no longer know much
About there. My experience has slipped away
There was in fact nothing to understand.
Oh this sleep-walking life of cats.
The past now like a sweep's brush.

Heumonat

Der Singschwan ist über den Strand
Weiter nach Norden geflogen
Wir vergessen die Dunkelheit die
So lange uns eingehüllt und verbiestert.

Und bald der Brachvogel schreit
Vom stillen Blumentod immer die
Nämliche Weise. Ich will
Nicht ins Haus gehn.

Hay month

The whooper swan flew over the strand
Farther north
We forget the darkness that
Engulfed us and made us grouchy for so long.

And soon the curlew squawks
About the quiet death of flowers
Always in the same way. I don't want
To go into the house.

Krähengeschwätz

Mein Richtstern ist ein faust-
Grosser Planet und mein Kompaß
Liegt auf dem Grund der See
Aber die Hoffnung will tanzen
Nur der Sperber über der Ebene
Liest die Gedanken.

Erde und Menschen sind
Gänzlich verwildert hilft
Kein Besinnen der Klotz
Ist unterwegs im freien Fall
Und ich selbst
Entstamme einer Familie von Wölfen.

The chitchat of crows

My guiding star is a planet
As big as a fist and my compass
Is lying on the bottom of the ocean
But hope wants to dance
Only the sparrowhawk above the lowlands
Can read thoughts.

Earth and folk
Have gone to rack and ruin
No thinking will help the block
Is on its way in free fall
And I myself
Am from a family of wolves.

From

Erlkönigs Tochter
(Alder King's Daughter)

Mauer

Bunt war sie hier Fenster und Türen
Aufmüpfige Leitern Ikarus-
Flügel schimärenhaft hingemalt an einer
Bestimmten Stelle auch ich nebst meinem
Unerschrockenen Kind wie wir eines Tages
Durch sie gekommen sind mit einem
Spielzeugkoffer woraus russische
Schwerter mongolische Kesselchen fielen
Einer Schreibmaschine die halbfertigen
Liebesgeschichten klemmten noch in der
Walze und ein paar freundliche
Karten von Elis und Franz er war es der mich
Noch zweimal besuchte vor er in Märkisch
Buchholz unter den Rasen geriet – ich schaute
Wohl nicht zurück übte weiter den
Kopf ordentlich schütteln sprang zu
Marine and Edith in den krachenden
Wagen unsere Schwestern gehen in
Bunten Kleidern zeigten mir einen
Papierweißen Garten zwischen Norden und
Nacht da lagen am Boden die
Königsmützen.

Wall

It was colourful here windows and doors
Rebellious ladders Icarus-
Wings painted on chimera-like
At a certain point me too beside
My brave child as we came through it
One day with a case of toys
Out of which fell Russian swords
Small Mongolian kettles
A typewriter with half-finished
Love stories still wedged in
The rollers and a couple of friendly
Cards from Elis and Franz that's the one
Who visited me twice more before he ended up
Under the grass in Buchholz Mark Brandenburg – I didn't
Look back of course kept practising
Shaking my head correctly dashed over
To Marina and Edith in the old
Banger our sisters go about
In bright clothes they showed me a
Paper-white garden between North and
Night where the kings' caps
Lay on the ground.

Später

Die Kerzen flackern im Garten
Während die Gäste sich
Langsam entfernen. Ich gehe
Als Bauer verkleidet hinter den
Hecken. Eine Vorbereitung auf
Etwas das niemals geschieht.

Later

The candles flicker in the garden
As the guests depart
Slowly. I go
Behind the hedge disguised
As a farmer. Getting ready for
Something that never happens.

Zwischen Heu und Gras

Zuerst muß man
Wollen der Rest ist
Technik zwischen Heu und
Gras fuhr ich im Linienbus
Der Wind heulte daß die
Ohren ertaubten ich wanderte
Über Moore durch schwimmige
Wiesen Schneeanemonen
Krochen mir in den Pelz
Braunschwarz das Ödland wien
Isländischer Abendkaffee
Runde Seen dazwischen
Erste schüchterne hungrige
Schafe und wie im Traum der
Leibhafte Gletscher.

Between hay and grass

Firstly you must
Want to the rest's
Engineering between hay and
Grass I went by bus
The wind howled so much
My ears turned numb I wandered
Over moors through spongy
Meadows snow anemones
Crawled inside my fur coat
Brown-black the wasteland like an
Icelandic evening coffee
Round lakes in between
The first shy hungry sheep
And as in a dream
The glacier incarnate.

Traum

Kam an der gotischen Insel vorüber
Die Stadtmauer war mit Rosen bespannt zärtlich
Erblühten Elke blickte hindurch sagte Konrad
Will Berufssoldat werden! Wie ist das
Möglich. Ob er der Wechselbalg ist? In solch
Einem Fall genügt es den Molotow-Cocktail
Kräftig zu schütteln bevor man das Feuerzeug
Dreht ist das Wesen verschwunden im
Korridor steht das richtige etwas größere
Kind und geht zum Zivildienst Vögel beringen.

Dream

Came to the Gothic island over which
The city wall was decked with roses blooming
Tenderly Elke looked through said Konrad
Wanted to be a professional soldier! How is
That possible. Is he perhaps the changeling? In cases
Like this it suffices to shake
The Molotov cocktail hard before you flick
The lighter the creature's disappeared
And the proper somewhat larger kid
Is standing in the hall volunteering
For community service ringing birds.

Watt I

Salzränder am Schuhwerk ich lief
Unterm Leuchtfeuer hin der Flutsaum
Setzt sich aus Meergras Möwenflügeln
Plastikgerümpel grämlich zusammen
Muschelgeld uralt dazwischen
Gestreut etliche Sterne.
Die Priele glitzern wien tiefes
Gedächtnis die schmale Sichel
Sich verpissenden Mondes ging
Im zerfledderten Himmel ich konnte
Die Füße nicht lösen und schlich
Als hätte mich Caspar Davids
Schlechterer Vetter
Mit Pech auf den Strand gemalt.
Von den Halligen tönte
Gänsegeschrei.

Mudflats I

Salt stains on my footwear I ran there
Under navigational light the tidal debris
Consists sullenly of seaweed seagulls' wings
Plastic junk shell-currency
From time immemorial several stars
Scattered in amongst it.
The narrow mudflats glitter
Like a sunken memory the slim sickle
Of the pissing-off moon was moving
In the tattered sky I could not
Free my feet and crawled
As if Caspar David's
Inferior cousin had
Painted me on sand with pitch
The cry of geese could be heard
From the Hallig Islands.

Watt II

Ich Erlkönigs Tochter hab eine
Ernsthafte Verabredung mit zwei
Apokalyptischen Reitern im Watt ein
Techtelmechtel auf unsicherem Boden
Jetzt ehe der Morgen sich rötet.

Drehender Nebelqualm bemerkenswert
Eiliger Schneefall stellen ne schöne
Verbindlichkeit her das legt sich
Auf Möwenkadaver Colabüchsen der
Abgeblaßte Mond auf der Hurtigroute
Zwischen kopulierenden Wolken bezeugt er
Dem Albatros höchste Bewunderung wie der
Von Süden herüberkömmt während Jupiter
Über dem Kuhstall später der Bohrinsel glänzt.
Happy Neujahr! Rufen die Seenotraketen
Und der Jung aus Büsum wird niemals
Gefunden es fallen die Krähen
Schwarze Äpfel vom einzigen Baum.

Mudflats II

I the Alder King's daughter have a
Serious appointment on the mudflats
With two apocalyptic horsemen an
Affair on shaky ground
Now before the morning turns red.
Remarkable swirling fog-smoke
Hurried snowfall call forth
A beautiful binding force that settles
On seagull carcasses cola cans
The wan moon on the Hurtig Route
Between copulating clouds receives
The albatross's highest admiration as he
Flies over from the south while Jupiter
Glistens above the byre later the drilling rig.
Happy New Year! call the sea rescue flares
And the boy from Büsum's never found
Crows black apples fall from the only tree.

Edelstein wird es genannt

Der Eisvogel verließ zum ersten
Mal das Nest flatterte in die
Zweige während hinter dem
Mühlstein die alte
Gewiefte Katze lauert. Vergeudung
Schöner Farben gerade erlernter
Anmut.

Jewel they call it

The kingfisher left the nest
For the first time flapped up
Into the branches while
The old curved cat lurks behind
The millstone. A waste
Of beautiful colours newly gained
Grace.

Geschöpfe

Es ist Nacht. Kilometerweit in der Ebene
Ein einzelnes Licht. Ich stelle mir
Menschen vor die es angeknipst haben
Eine vollzählige kurzweilige Großfamilie
Und verschiedene Beweggründe dazu Liebe
Eifersucht Wahnsinn und Tod. Es könnte
Auch eine Tiergeburt sein sehr
Wahrscheinlich in solcher Gegend zu
Dieser Zeit. Alles erwägend die Möglichkeiten
Durchgehend und ist es ein Kalb oder ein
Schwein welchen Geschlechts oder ein
Mischling – die großzügig ausgestatteten
Bewohner des Hauses des Stalles die
Besitzer des Lichts bleiben Gegenstand
Meiner Sorge bis ihre Lampe wieder
Erlischt. Dann sind sie mir alle
Gestorben.

Creatures

It is night. Miles away on the plain
A single light. I imagine
People who have switched it on
An entertaining large family all there
And various reasons including love
Jealousy madness and death. It might
Also be an animal birth very likely
In a place like this at this time.
Weighing everything sifting
Possibilities is it a calf or a
Pig which sex or is it a
Half-breed – the handsomely resourced
Inhabitants of the house the cowshed
The owners of the light concern me
Until their lamp goes out
Then for me they're all
Dead.

Engel

Bevor ich meine
Eigenen Unwahrheiten
In Stein haue oder
In die gefrorene
Erde säe:

Dein Haus steht am
Weltrand ich gehe
Durch seinen leeren Garten.
Das Fenster brennt rot
Ich bin totenblaß wie
Gefallener Schnee.

Angels

Before I carve
My own untruths
In stone or
Sow them
In the frozen ground:

Your house stands
At the edge of the world I go
Through its empty garden.
The window burns red
I am pale as death
Like fallen snow.

Kalt

Aus teerschwarzem Meer steigt der
Mond auf. Solltest nun
Unter ein Dach gelangen verehrtes
Herz. Sonst greint die Sehnsucht
Ihren verlorenen Traum von der
Schönheit der Welt die so
Verkommen darnieder
Liegt. Blatt geht weil Frost
Andere Zeit macht.

Cold

From a pitch-black sea the moon
Is rising. You should now
Seek cover dear
Heart. Otherwise longing will howl
Your lost dream
Of the beauty of the world
That languishes so debauchedly.
The leaf falls because frost
Heralds a new time.

Freie Verse

Gestern Nacht erwachte ich wußte
Daß ich mich nun von diesen Versen
Verabschieden sollte. So geht es immer
Nach einigen Jahren. Sie müssen hinaus
In die Welt. Es ist nicht möglich sie
Ewig! hier unter dem Dach zu behalten.
Arme Dinger. Sie müssen hin in die Stadt.
Wenige werden später zurückkommen dürfen.
Jedoch die meisten treiben sich draußen herum.
Wer weiß was aus ihnen noch wird. Eh sie
Zur Ruhe gelangen.

Free verse

Last night I woke up knew
That I should now part
With these verses. That happens
Every few years. They must go out
Into the world. It's not possible
To keep them sheltered here forever!
Poor things. They must go into town.
A few will be able to return later on.
But most of them will knock about out there.
Who knows what will become of them.
Before they come to rest.

From

Bodenlos
(Fathomless)

Ruß

Die Touristen sind letzlich
Gestorben. Ich habe Lust durch die
Sümpfe zu gehen. Gänseschwarm
Lange gezogen. Schneegestöber
Aus der Tür offenen Kühlschranks.
Benzin- und Whisky-Büchsen
Pfeifender redender Wind.

Soot

The tourists have just bitten
The dust. I feel like walking
Through the swamps. A long-
Drawn-out flock of geese. Snow drifts
Out of the door of the open fridge.
Little tins of petrol and whisky
Whistling speaking wind.

Alles Spatzen und Gänseblümchen

Im Mondlicht hör ich
Stolpern und Fallen.
Man hat den
Tischler Maß nehmen
Lassen. O die

Dunkelheit dauert und
Dauert. Falls ich den

Sommer erlebe lebe ich
Tanzend.

It's all sparrows and daisies

In the moonlight I hear
Stumbling and falling.
They have let
The joiner measure
Up. Oh the

Darkness lasts and
Lasts. If I

Live to see the summer
I will dance through life.

Seestück

Ich bin die
Mutter der auf dem
Meer segelnden
Söhne warte am
Strand mit den
Zündhölzern in der
Schnürzentasche.

Sea piece

I'm the mother
Of the sons sailing
On the ocean waiting
On the shore with
Matches in my
Apron pocket.

Bodenlos

Wohne seit langem am Boden
Der Flüße. Die Schwäne
Rudern über das Blau. Siehst du
Ihn noch? Fragt mich die
Ralle. Ja überall.

Fathomless

I've been living for a long time on the bottom
Of rivers. The swans
Row across the blue. Do you
Still see him? The rail asks me.
Yes wherever I look.

Espresso

Wo ist der Zucker die Milch – ist denn
Gar nichts vorbereitet hier? Man kommt
Nach zwei Monaten und nichts
Ist in Ordnung. Wo denn
Orion der Halbmond die Eule? Wieso
Hat sich der alte Kater
Die Pfote gebrochen?

Espresso

Where is the sugar the milk has nothing
Been prepared here at all? You return
After two months and nothing
Is in order. Where's Orion
The half-moon the owl? How did
The old tom-cat
Break his paw?

Sonnen

Jetzt wo der Sommer gleich
Kommt habe ich gar keine
Sonne. Aber im Winter
Im härtesten Winter hatte ich
Deren soviel ich nur wollte.
Einmal standen sieben am
Himmel machten einen
Orion für mich.

Suns

Now that summer's just
About to begin
I don't have any sun
At all. But in winter
In the hardest winter
I had as much as I could wish for.
Once there were seven in the sky
Creating for me my own Orion.

Crusoe

Es gibt ihn den
Charme hier der
Einsamkeit etwas
Wovon niemand mehr
Weiß der die Schreiberin
Aufs höchste ermutigt wenn die
Abnehmende Welt immer
Schneller versinkt deren
Verdienst es ist das
Grün zu verspotten.

Mein grün Gefängnis es schenkt
Außerordentlich Freude die
Füchsin fürchtet mich nicht
Vögel lachen wenn ich Crusoe
Meine eigenen Felder bestelle.
Oder die Eichen
Mit ihren Früchten mich wecken.

Crusoe

Here there is
The charm of solitude
Something no one
Knows any longer
Which strongly encourages
The female writer
When the waning world
Whose contribution it has been
To ridicule the green
Is sinking ever faster.

My green prison gives
Enormous pleasure the vixen
Does not fear me
Birds laugh when I Crusoe
Till my own fields.
Or when the oaks
Wake me with their fruits.

Flügelschlag

Meine Jungsteinzeit denke ich geht nun
Zuende. Ich werfe den Faustkeil
Achtlos zur Seite bediene mich
Raffinierterer Bronzefeder notiere
Seltsamen Lebensweg von mir
Selbst überflogen von
Herrlichen Wolken grauen
Wackelndem Reiher der jetzt
Niedergeht damit die
Landschaft vollständig würde.

Flap of the wing

My Neolithic Age is now ending
I believe. I toss the biface axe
Aside carelessly avail myself
Of slick bronze quills record
My own strange journey
Through life overflown by
Wonderful greying clouds
The wobbling heron
That now comes down
To finish the picture.

Dezember

Kein Baum kein
Strauch. Düsterer Sumpf.
Düsterer Sumpf und sonst
Gar nichts –

Verfaulte Boote am
Grund. Fischköpfe
Stotternde Katzen.

December

No tree no
Bush. A gloomy swamp.
A gloomy swamp and nothing
Else at all –

Rotten boats on
Land. Fish heads
Stuttering cats.

Bestürzungen

Man bemerkt spät daß der
Winter hereinbrach.
Irgendeine
Mondnacht hinterläßt
Weiße bereifte Pflanzen.
Und falls du dich nun
Nach Kummer sehnst hast du
Die ganze Welt Söhnchen.

Consternations

We notice late on
That winter has begun.
Some moonlit night
Leaves white
Frosted plants behind.
And if you're now longing
For problems sonny
The whole world's your oyster.

Arbeit

Oder meine driftenden Inseln im
Nordlicht die klein sind absolut
Nutzlos weshalb ich mich sehr um sie
Sorge der einen Schilf muß geschnitten
Werden die andre gepflügt die jüngste
Trieb über den Horizont zu den
Inselfressern daß ich verknoteter Zunge
Sie heimholen muß wiedererlangen sie

Ist es die jetzt profundeste
Weltuntergänge zu bieten hat schön!
Aber ich habe beschlossen über sie
Nichts mehr zu sagen weil sie
Die liebste ja ist. Bei den
Übrigen kümmre ich mich
Um Pirole Eruptionen und
Ameisenberge.

Work

Or my floating islands in
The aurora borealis that are small completely
Pointless which is why I take good care
Of them on the one reeds must be cut
The other must be ploughed the youngest
Drifted across the horizon to the
Island munchers and I with knotted tongue
Must fetch it home recover it

If this is now the most profound
Of armageddons on offer that's fine!
But I've decided to say nothing
More about it since
It's the one I love most. When it comes
To the others my worries are
Orioles eruptions and
Mountains of ants.

Jahresende

Föhn dreht den
See um stellt einen
Zauberspiegel vor die
Schwarzweißen Alpen daß ich dich
Sehe bis zu den
Knien im Tyrrhenischen
Meer so entfernt so
Rausgeschnitten

End of the year

Foehn inverts
The lake places a
Magic mirror before
The black-white Alps so I can see
You up to your knees
In the Tyrrhenian Sea
So distant so
Crystal clear

Franziskus

Wie Natur auf ihre Art sich uns
Mitteilt redet er in seiner Sprache
Zu ihren Wesen das bricht
Vulkanisch aus seinem Körper die
Rede ist lang eindringlich feurig von
Reiner Gebärde begleitet im räudigen
Stadtpark von Feldafing ein Brunnen
Dem man das Maul gestopft hat fünf
Elende geköpfte Bäume im Schnee
Er sprach ihnen Schönheit und Mut zu
Würde der funkelnde Sommer herannahm
Berufsnachtigallen für ihre Schöpfe
Die vorübergehenden Menschen
Senkten die Blicke der beschnittenste
Baum fuhr ein haltbares Blatt aus

Francis

Just as nature lets us know
In her own way he speaks in his
To her creatures language bursts
Volcanically from his body the
Speech is long insistent fiery
Accompanied by pure gestures in
The mangy town park of Feldafing
He conferred beauty and courage
On a fountain whose gob had been stuffed
And on five wretched trees that lay beheaded in the snow
By saying that as the glowing summer approached
They'd have professional nightingales for their crowns
The passing people looked down
The most pruned-back tree
Produced a durable leaf

From

Schwanenliebe

(Swan Love)

Dreierlei

Engel über den
Himmel geblasen.

Die Grüben voller
Schwanenblumen.

Einer Krähe
Schönheit.

Wolken wie
Treue Hunde warten
Auf mich wir wissen
Nicht wohin wir
Gehen wenn wir erst
Losgegangen sind.

Die Häuser
Strecken sich in den
Abend. Der Wind
Galoppiert die
Straße hinauf und
Herunter kleine
Laternen
Schütteln.

Three sorts of

Angels blown
Across the sky.

Road ditches full of
Flowering rush.

The beauty
Of a crow.

Clouds like faithful
Dogs wait
For me we
Don t know where
We are going when we
First set out.

The houses
Stretch into the
Evening. The wind
Gallops up and
Down the
Street small
Lanterns
Shake.

Bist durch die
Wiesen die
Aufgestellten
Kühe geschritten.
Zart wie geträumte
Liebe die
Regenfinger.

Trauer hier
Ist dein Platz.

Bleib ruh
Aus
Schönes Gesicht.

Ich hab Brennesseln
Gezogen
Mit Samthandschuhn
Fragst du im
Samttelefon.

Die Schwestern die
Kühe auf
Hackenschuhen
Sie sind
Vorübergegangen oh
Bruder Hund begleite
Mich heute.

You walked
Through the fields
The cows in
Fixed position.
Dainty as day-dreamed
Love rain-
Fingers.

Grief your place
Is here.

Stay and
Rest
Lovely face.

I pulled nettles
With velvet
Gloves you ask
Down the velvet
Telephone.

The sisters the
Cows on
Heeled shoes
Have gone
Past oh
Brother dog stay
By me today.

Öffnen

Kam Sonne hellgelbes
Haar.

Am Abend jagt der
Wind Flügel
An die
Stämme der
Pappeln.

Du denkst an deine
Unbekannte Liebe
Mit der du so
Lange glücklich
Schon lebst.

Wolken in
Umstandskleidern zwischen
Frühling und Sommer. Die weiße
Kuh mit der Maske
Geht am Fenster vorbei.

Kaum ziehst du den
Handschuh aus du mit solchen
Fingern worauf Bienen und
Käfer landen sich
Tragen zu lassen.

Opening

Sun came bright yellow
Hair.

In the evening the
Wind chases wings
Against the
Poplar tree
Trunks.

You think of your
Unknown love
With whom you've
Lived happily for
So long.

Clouds in
Maternity clothes
Between spring and summer. The white
Cow with the mask
Goes past the window.

You hardly take off
Your glove you with such
Fingers on which bees and
Bugs land and
Let themselves be carried.

Nördliche
Sommernächte die
Von allen Seiten zu
Kurz sind schauen
Zehen hervor.

Solch leichtes Land der Wind
Weht es in Sandsäulen fort.

Das samtschöne
Schieferblau am
Abend.

Die Singschwäne fliegen
Der Mond scheint lange
Hinter ihnen her.

Northern
Summer nights which
Are too short
From all sides
When toes stick out.

Such light land the wind
Blows it away in pillars of sand.

The velveteen
Slate blue of
Evening.

The whooper swans fly
The moon shines after them
For a long time.

Seit du fort bist

Bin ich in einem
Verödeten Haus mit
Spinnen und Fliegen
Stürzen die Rosenblätter.

Wenn es beiläufig donnert und
Blitze wie Lassos schwingen bist du
Womöglich im Haus schreibst
Ein Blatt Schwanentreue.

Since you've been gone

I am in
A deserted house with
Spiders and flies
Nose-diving into rose leaves.

When thunder casually crashes
And lightning flashes swing like lassos
You're possibly at home writing
A page with swan-like loyalty.

Jäger

Der Reiher steht auf
Einem Fuß im
Wasser den anderen
Erhoben mit gedrehtem
Hals. Er blickt dich an.

Hunter

The heron stands on
One foot in the
Water the other lifted
Up his neck con-
Torted. He looks at you.

Andenken

Grün stehen die vom
Fremden niedergemachten
Pappeln in deinen Augen.

Memento

In your eyes the poplar trees
Slaughtered by a stranger
Are still standing green.

Mond

Neu ist er.
Gepiercte Nacht.

Moon

It is new.
Pierced night.

November

Dann schreit die ganze
Dachkante im schneidenden
Wind und der herrliche
Falke sitzt auf der
Erde wo schwarze
Stiere gestanden sind.

Das letzte Vieh
Wirft lange Schatten.

Das kann ich
Schwören daß es hier
Ein Pferd gibt das
Dich in keinen
Hinterhalt trägt.

Hier kenne ich
Nur eine Erle
Graugans aus
Luft jetzt bin ich
Überall.

November

Then the entire roof-edge
Cries in the biting wind
And the splendid
Falcon sits
On the earth
Where black bulls stood.

The last animal
Casts long shadows.

I can promise
That here there is
A horse that will
Not carry you
Into an ambush.

Here I know
Only an alder
Grey goose of air
Now I am
Everywhere.

Manchmal konnte ich
Schwäne heranschaun
Ein einziges Mal einen
Kometen was
Glänzten die Augen.

Tag Tag aller
Schönster Tag wie
Dunkelheit aus dem
Kasten steigt ein rotes
Stück Mond aufgeht
Kupferglucken Silber
Mönche Zimtbären
Achateulen durchs
Fenster.

Sometimes I could
Look at swans
Just once a meteor
Whose eyes
Were gleaming.

Day day the most
Beautiful day like
Darkness from a
Box a red slice
Of moon is rising
Copper lappet silver
Scarce prominent ruby tiger
Angle shade moths
Through the window.

Advent

Drei Fenster geöffnet
In einer Sprechblase einen
Seufzer gefunden.

Nein nein keine
Luftpost kein
Erdstoß kein
Wasserzeichen
Nein nichts nur
Patagonische Kälte.

Das Laub wird aus
Großer Entfernung
Zusammengeblasen die
Sonne schlurft in
Sandalen.

Advent

Three windows opened
In one speech bubble
I discovered a sigh.

No no no
Airmail no
Seismic shock
No water mark
No nothing only
Patagonian cold.

The leaves are blown
Together from
A great distance the sun
Shuffles about
In sandals.

Aussicht

Der Mond ein
Däne nackt und
Rosa kommt er
Aus der Eider.

Ein Schwan der auf
Gold schwimmt.

Die Schere will sich nicht
Öffnen zum Rosenschneiden.

View

The moon a
Dane naked and
Pink when it comes
Out of the Eider.

A swan that
Swims on gold.

The scissors won't open
To cut the rose.

Falken

Schlecht gelaunt sind wir
Außer uns nur Spatzen
In der Voliere.

Die Krähen zu
Hören über dem
Schwarzen Fluß.

Graue Sonne
Die Krähe hackt
Den Schnee.

Hellrote Bänder nachts
Am Horizont hinter
Geduckten Bäumen ein
Schwanenschrei.

Schwarze
Himmelsfalten ich schaue
Auf den gebogenen
Schwappenden
Styx.

Falcon

We're not very happy
Apart from us
Only sparrows in the sanctuary.

To hear crows
Above
The black river.

Grey sun
The crow pecks
The snow.

Bright red ribbons at night
On the horizon
Behind crouching trees
A swan's screech.

Black sky-
Pleats I look on-
To the curved,
Swashing
Styx.

Epitaph

Ging in Güllewiesen als sei es
Das Paradies beinahe verloren im
Märzen der Bauer hatte im
Herbst sich erhängt.

Epitaph

Walked in Güllewiesen as if it
Was paradise almost lost in
March the farmer had hanged
Himself in the autumn.

Index of Titles and First Lines (English)

Titles are in italic, first lines in roman type.

Index of Titles and First Lines (German)

Titles are in italic, first lines in roman type.

INDEX OF TITLES AND FIRST LINES (GERMAN) 267